THE RISK OF DISCIPLESHIP

Also by Roderick Strange

The Catholic Faith
Living Catholicism

Praise for *The Catholic Faith*

'[Roderick Strange] is loyal to the Church's dogmatic and moral teaching, yet the whole work is shot through with living theology. It is based both on his deep knowledge of the Catholic faith and on his own pastoral experience of people's needs, as his fund of real-life stories in the book testifies.' *The Universe*

'Here is a coherently expounded faith which appeals to both heart and head, a theology which leads into prayer and a praying which is solidly founded.' *The Tablet*

Praise for *Living Catholicism*

'Particularly compelling is how Strange portrays Jesus as fully human, without compromising the Christian conviction that Jesus was also the son of God. That ability to affirm the faith in its fullness . . . without falling back on the ponderous formulation of the dogmatic theologians is one of the more attractive aspects of this work.' *Commonweal*

'*Living Catholicism* is beautifully written: clear, elegant, simple, with enlightening personal anecdotes . . . Apart from its style, the spiritual/doctrinal combination is very effective. Reading it, chapter by chapter, was rather like making a retreat.' Margaret Small, Former Director of the Catholic Education Service

THE RISK OF DISCIPLESHIP

The Catholic Priest Today

RODERICK STRANGE

First published in 2004 by
Darton, Longman and Todd Ltd
1 Spencer Court
140–142 Wandsworth High Street
London SW18 4JJ

ISBN 0–232–52512–9

A catalogue record for this book is available from the
British Library.

Designed by Sandie Boccacci
Phototypeset in 11¼/14pt Bembo by
Intype Libra Limited, London
Printed and bound in Great Britain by
Page Bros, Norwich, Norfolk

Contents

For
Andrew Faley
and
Mark Coleridge.

Acknowledgements

SOME of the ideas included in this book have appeared in articles I have written elsewhere. I am grateful to *Priests and People*, *The Tablet*, and *The Times* for allowing me to adapt the material for use here.

I wish also to record my thanks to Lord Mark Saville, Lord of Appeal in Ordinary, for allowing me to quote from his address at the Memorial Service for Professor Barry Nicholas.

Quotations from the documents of the Second Vatican Council come from the edition by Austin Flannery OP (Dublin, 1975).

Preface

WHEN Brendan Walsh approached me and asked whether I would write a book about priesthood for Darton, Longman and Todd, I replied at once that I had no interest in concentrating more or less exclusively on controversial questions. Others have written elsewhere wisely and well about sexual scandals, falling numbers, optional celibacy, the ordination of married men, the ordination of women, the proportion of homosexuals who have been ordained, and the future of ordained ministry. The literature is extensive. I did not feel I could add to it usefully. Brendan agreed. He had something else in mind and it was the very idea which had already appealed to me.

As a seminary rector, I have become aware of a gap in the literature on priesthood. When people approach us – all too rarely at the moment, as may be – and tell us they are wondering whether they have a vocation to priesthood and asking for something to read, what do we suggest? There are splendid books on various aspects of priesthood, especially on its theology and on spirituality. Some are wonderfully accessible. I am thinking particularly of Tony Philpot's powerful, slim volumes, *Brothers in Christ*, *Priesthood in Reality*, and *You Shall Be Holy*,[1] and Tom Lane's more ambitious work, *A Priesthood in Tune*.[2] But many others are technical and may seem forbidding and too detailed for someone beginning to explore. That, first of all, is the gap I have tried to fill. I am hoping that this is a book, not too long nor too daunting, which can be put in the hands of those who are trying to discern their vocation for themselves.

1. Tony Philpot, *Brothers in Christ* (Rattlesden, 1991); *Priesthood in Reality* (Rattlesden, 1998); *You Shall Be Holy* (Buxhall, 2003).
2. Thomas Lane CM, *A Priesthood in Tune: Theological Reflections on Ministry* (Dublin, 1993).

But I am not writing for them alone. There are other people who may have no wish to be ordained, but who wish to understand this vocation and ministry better. They enjoy reading, but are too busy to work their way through an entire shelf of books. However, they would appreciate a work which distils into a single chapter key ideas on the main aspects of priestly life such as prayer, celibacy, scholarship, and pastoral ministry. I hope they will find their need addressed here.

I would like to think as well that this book will encourage and support those who have already been ordained. Buffeted by controversy and with so many demands made on them, I hope they may discover in what I write a cheering reminder of the call that has prompted them to walk this path. However rocky the road and in spite of stumbling sometimes, those who have remained faithful have cause for rejoicing.

The book passes through various stages. We must begin with Jesus of Nazareth. He is the one who supplies us irreplaceably with the model of our ministry. He is our master and friend, and the brother above all others who reveals to us the risk of discipleship by accepting death on the cross. He surrendered control in order to obey his Father's will. Then when we study our vocation in the light of who he was and what he did, we find that the model he offers has been interpreted with various emphases throughout the course of the Christian centuries. That very variety has lessons to teach us and it helps us to reflect more deeply on what it means to be a presbyter. We clarify the distinction between the common and the ministerial priesthood.

When that has been established, we can consider first different aspects of a priest's interior life. Sane humanity is the indispensable basis for this ministry. Moreover, as mature human beings, we are called to be people who love. We must recognize that that love is compatible with being celibate. We must also be people who do not merely say prayers, but who live prayerfully. And as the spirit needs prayer, so the mind needs study. We must value learning so as to account for the hope that is in us. Maturity, the courage to love, a commitment to prayer, and enthusiasm for study, these are vital aspects of a priest's interior life. They equip us for our ministry: we must preach the gospel, celebrate the sacramental mysteries, and offer a style of leadership rooted in service like the Son of man who came not to be served, but to serve. Such is the ministry we offer and in which we are called to persevere. Ours is to be an enduring commitment. That in brief is the route this work follows.

Various themes run through it like threads. One is the attempt to clarify the distinction between the common priesthood of all the baptized and the ministerial priesthood of those who have been ordained. A second is the discovery of the identity of the ordained as a reality to be found within the community, not by separation from it: but what is asked of the baptized is expected of the ordained. And a third, the unifying idea which gives the book its title, is the risk of discipleship. Any significant decision involves risks, because we can never be certain what will happen. When we decide to take an initiative, we run risks, but they are in a way risks of our own choosing. When, however, we accept a vocation, we do not choose the risks we run; instead we accept the consequences, whatever they may be. This is the risk of discipleship and it recurs again and again.

It is obvious that so broad a treatment cannot be exhaustive. Someone else would handle the material differently. These, however, are key reflections which occur to me after more than thirty-three years as a Catholic priest. It is a life I have loved. The people, whether living or dead, whom you will meet in these pages and who help me illustrate what I am trying to explain, are mainly my friends. I owe them a debt of immeasurable gratitude.

I must thank others as well, especially Brendan Walsh for the invitation to put these ideas on paper, and Helen Porter, Rachel Davis and Eleanor Fletcher, his colleagues at Darton, Longman and Todd, who have encouraged and helped me. Brendan suggested wisely that what I wrote should be seen by a variety of people and I have pressed a range of my friends into service. Their advice has been invaluable. I have tried to include as much of it as possible and what remains unsatisfactory is obviously my fault, not theirs. My victims were Margaret Atkins, John Breen, Richard Dunleavy, Philip Endean, Andrew Faley, Nicholas King, Daniel Pakenham, Jim O'Keefe, Eileen Plunkett, Tony Philpot, Philippe Taupin, and Peter Taylor. I thank them all without reserve. Busy people, they have given valuable time to this enterprise.

This material has taken shape over the years in homilies and talks and lectures and retreats. I thank gladly those whom I have tried to serve in Bebington and Wallasey, in Hyde and Oxford. I remember happily retreats to the Basilians in Toronto and to the clergy of the Archdiocese of Southwark, and the Dioceses of Portsmouth, Hexham and Newcastle, and Brentwood in England. And I thank especially the staff and students of the Beda College and the Franciscan Missionaries of the Divine Motherhood who since my appointment here have helped me to deepen further my appreciation of my vocation. During that time Andrew Faley and Mark Coleridge have offered me in a particular way unfailing friendship and support. This book is dedicated to them.

Pontifical Beda College, Rome
20 September 2003

1

Recovering Lost Ground

(i)

THERE are various reasons for writing about Catholic priesthood at this time. Priesthood is an honourable way of life, but scandals and allegations of scandal have dishonoured it. There is plenty of evidence for that. A priest I know called in at his local supermarket and held the door open, as he arrived, for a woman who was leaving. He had never seen her before. She looked at him, stopped, and spat in his face. 'People like you should be in hell,' she told him. And Donald Cozzens in his book, *The Changing Face of Priesthood*, tells the story of a young man who was talking to a priest after mass one Sunday about his interest in priesthood. The priest had some literature with him and so gave it to the man. 'Suddenly,' Cozzens writes, 'his mother stood between them and grabbed the pamphlet from her son's hand. Throwing it down, she said with a voice of steel, "No son of mine is going to be a damn priest." Perhaps surprised at her own vehemence, she added, "Nothing against you, Father. It's just that no son of mine is going to be a priest." '[1] In these circumstances it is easy to become discouraged and demoralized. The wretched evil perpetrated by a few can undermine us all. But priesthood remains an honourable way of life. What can we do? A well-tried strategy comes to mind.

For twelve years I had the good fortune to work as a Catholic chaplain at Oxford University. During that time many people

1. Donald B. Cozzens, *The Changing Face of Priesthood* (Minnesota, 2000), p. 134.

who were not Catholics came to see me – graduates and undergraduates, dons and other members of the University and their families – to talk about the Catholic faith and explore the possibility of their becoming Catholics themselves. It was fascinating and rewarding work. Sometimes after a long series of sessions people might decide not to proceed. I never regarded it as time wasted. At least they would have clarified their own position and after all faith is a gift. And sometimes people were in more of a hurry. Occasionally someone would say, 'Look, I'm sure that I want to be received. I believe what the Church teaches. So could I be received soon? Perhaps we could just have a few sessions on the controversial issues, like the real presence of Christ in the eucharist, papal infallibility, and the teaching about Mary.' But I would always refuse. To examine only the problem issues can easily distort our understanding of the whole. More often, someone who had announced that transubstantiation or infallibility or Marian doctrine might be a sticking point, found when we reached that stage in our conversations that seen in context the difficulties had evaporated. I remember one person, now a friend, smiling wryly and expressing mock disappointment when we came to consider Mary. 'I was looking forward to a really good argument about that,' she said.

The point is significant here as we begin this reflection on Catholic priesthood. There are many controversial issues today surrounding it, not only the scandals arising from the sexual abuse of children. Why are so few people in Western Europe, the United States, and Australia recognizing a vocation as presbyters? Why have so many priests left the priesthood? Should celibacy remain obligatory? Should other married men, besides convert clergy, be ordained? Should women be ordained? What should be said about sexual orientation? And then there are the scandals that have engulfed priests time and again in more recent years. Those are some of the questions which are raised constantly. They deserve to be considered, although they have already received thoughtful attention in church documents, as well as in a range of books and articles. However, I want to offer an account of Catholic ministerial priesthood which is not governed by those issues. I have no wish to shy away from them, but would rather address them as they may arise, integrated within a larger view.

By doing so I would hope to encourage and support those who have become dispirited, informing people and reminding priests about what this commitment entails. I want to offer an account which allows the sheer goodness of this way of life to be acknowledged once more. It would be wonderful too if anything written here helped someone recognize a call to this life which until now they have not identified. And I am prompted to write partly because of a minor coincidence.

There is a common tradition that Jesus of Nazareth was thirty-three years old when he was crucified and I have now been a priest for thirty-three years, as long as Jesus lived. The coincidence is as tenuous as that, but they are years for which I can only be grateful. It seems in its way a good moment for me to pause and reflect; and if I am to share what I may have learnt with others, it may help if I begin by sketching my background and how those years have been spent.

(ii)

My family was Catholic and the faith was important in our home. My father had decided to become a Catholic before marrying my mother in 1939, but the wise Jesuit who was instructing him advised delay until after the wedding to spare his parents' feelings. Was that symbolic? The commitment was clear, but neither narrow nor rigid.

I went to school at Stonyhurst. There was a large number of Jesuits on the staff at the time and during those years the possibility of my becoming a priest occurred to me. I didn't cling to it desperately. If my mind had changed, I wouldn't have been devastated. But I came to realize it was a notion I ought to explore. On reflection I felt drawn to the diocesan priesthood rather than the Society of Jesus. I applied to my home diocese of Shrewsbury and was accepted. I was sent to Rome and began my studies in 1963. I was seventeen.

Today that seems extraordinary, far too young. But things were different in the sixties. When people left school in those days, they had usually decided what they wanted to do with their lives. And it was an exceptional time to be in Rome.

Each autumn of my first three years the Second Vatican Council was sitting. When documents were to be promulgated, there were public sessions and I attended as many as I could. They were wonderful days. There was a sense of being part of historic events. And the years which followed were as absorbing in a different way. In the immediate aftermath of the Council the flow of visitors to Rome continued; they were attending sessions of the post-conciliar commissions which were seeking to put what the Council had taught into effect. It was a privileged time to be training for the priesthood and it has shaped my life. The Council's vision inspires me.

I was ordained a priest of the Shrewsbury Diocese in December 1969 and after my return from Rome the following June, I was sent to Oxford to study Newman. I lived at the University Catholic Chaplaincy for the next four years. Crispian Hollis, now the Bishop of Portsmouth, was chaplain. He had just succeeded Michael Hollings who in the previous eleven years had transformed the place. He had established it as an open house and Crispian maintained the practice. The doors were unlocked at seven in the morning and closed at midnight. It was an inspiring model of priesthood to meet in my formative years. And at its heart was prayerfulness. The early mass was said at 7.45 in the morning in a small upstairs chapel, but a good half-hour before that fifteen or more people would have gathered to prepare themselves in silence. You could set your clock by Bill Frerking, an American philosophy graduate, who had had polio as a child, climbing those stairs on his crutches at 7.10. He is now a Benedictine abbot in the United States.[2]

I left Oxford in 1974 and returned as one of the Catholic chaplains to the University in 1977. During those three years I was an assistant priest in a parish, English Martyrs in Wallasey, and also chaplain to the large Catholic comprehensive school, St Mary's College, which is next door. After Oxford, when I returned to the diocese in 1990, I was appointed parish priest of St Paul's, Hyde, and in 1993 I became Director of the Diocesan Religious Education Service for five years. I also spent eight years as a member of the National Conference of Priests and served as its chairman from 1994 to 1997. I had been moved from Hyde back to Wallasey in 1996 to facilitate the R.E. work and then in 1998 I was invited to return to Rome as Rector of the Beda College which has the responsibility of preparing for priestly ordination older men from the English-speaking world. The invitation could not have surprised me more.

Parish and school, university and seminary, and like all priests a variety of other responsibilities besides, my years as a priest have offered me a range of experience and that experience is one of the sources on which I draw and reflect here. This book is not, however, disguised autobiography, but having had the experience, in Eliot's phrase, I don't want to miss the meaning.[3] And I would want to state something clearly from the start. I have loved being a priest.

During my time as a student in Rome I became friendly with Jack Pledger, a priest from the Archdiocese of Southwark, who used to come out on holiday. I learnt a great deal from him. By his own admission Jack did not suffer fools gladly, but he had great zest for living. 'What's the point of being a priest,' he would say, 'if you're not going to be happy about it.' His own

2. See Roderick Strange, 'Michael Hollings at Oxford', in Jock Dalrymple, Joan McCrimmon, and Terry Tastard (eds.), *Press On! Michael Hollings, his Life and Witness* (Great Wakering, 2001), pp. 89–99.
3. See T.S. Eliot, 'Dry Salvages' II, *The Four Quartets*.

delight in priesthood was transparent. And it was because of him that the card commemorating my ordination bore the simple statement, 'Serve the Lord with joy.' I have tried to be faithful to those words. So what path shall we follow now?

(iii)

The fundamental theme for these reflections is the risk of discipleship. The very idea of risk is fascinating. Risks do not fall into a single category. There is a distinction between the risks we run because we have ourselves taken an initiative and those we face because we have accepted an invitation. Let's call them respectively the risks of initiative and the risks of invitation.

When we take an initiative – for example, to move house or change job or emigrate – we assess the implications. We weigh the pros and cons, we consider the advantages and disadvantages. We know we don't control the outcome. The conclusion is uncertain. Some risk is unavoidable. If we decide to proceed, however, the risks can be described as of our own choosing. They are our risks. On the other hand, when we receive an invitation, we know that that too involves risks. We don't know precisely what will happen. Once again, we look ahead and weigh up whether or not to accept. We think it through as best we can. And if we accept, it's our decision and we must take responsibility for it. But I would suggest that, if we accept, the risks involved are different from those which are part of an initiative we may take. The risks which come from accepting an invitation are not as such of our own choosing. When we accept an invitation, we make a commitment, and so we accept the risks, the consequences of that commitment, whatever they may be. Calculation is utterly foreign to such commitment.

In the Synoptic Gospels, at the start of his public ministry people gathered around Jesus. We learn about two pairs of brothers, Simon and Andrew, James and John, who were fishermen. He called them and they left everything, boats, nets, livelihood, and followed him (see Mark 1:16–20). In the Fourth

Gospel the story is told differently. There John the Baptist points Jesus out to two of his disciples, one of whom is Andrew. They approach him and ask, 'Rabbi, where are you staying?' He replies, 'Come and see.' And they spend the day with him. Andrew then looks for his brother, Simon Peter, and the following day Jesus finds Philip who in turn brings Nathanael to him (see John 1:37–51). These men will all become apostles, his closest disciples, but it is essential to appreciate what is happening.

It is not as though they have noticed this man from Nazareth and weighed the consequences of following him. They are not like entrepreneurs, calculating a risk which might make their future more profitable. They have not taken the initiative. Jesus has. He has called them, invited them, to follow him and they have responded. By that response they begin to run the risk of discipleship, the risk of invitation, not the risk of initiative.

And to be ordained is to accept an invitation. It is not my own initiative. At the Last Supper we hear Jesus telling his disciples, 'You did not choose me, but I chose you' (John 15:16). We have been called. We have received an invitation and answered, 'Yes.' Now we must run the risks which that acceptance involves, face the consequences of our commitment. The risk of discipleship, the theme which runs through these reflections and unifies them, refers to risks which are not of our choosing. That is what makes them the risks of discipleship. Lifelong commitment is not fashionable these days, but once committed, I accept whatever may be asked of me.

This life may be costly, but we must not be afraid. Nor must we fall prey to the lure of perfectionism, which will undermine us. From that viewpoint, we do not need to be perfect; it is sufficient to be good enough. We need, however, the courage to live at depth. Do we dare to do that? It may seem intimidating, but is also inspiring.

A short while ago I came across a passage from John Dunne's book *Time and Myth*, in which he speaks of an enduring life which lasts through and beyond death. 'To find [this deeper life than the ordinary]', he says, 'would be like seeing something fiery in the depths of life; it would be like hearing a rhythm in life that is not ordinarily heard.' I found myself wondering whether it could be taken as well to refer to the life to which a priest is called. He goes on:

> The question is whether a man, if he found such a life, could bear to live it, whether he could live at that depth, whether he could live according to that rhythm. The deeper life would be like an undertow, like a current that flows beneath the surface, a current that sets seaward or along the beach while the waves on the surface are breaking upon the shore . . . A life lived on the surface is like the surf itself, like the swell of the sea that breaks upon the shore, like the foam, the splash, the sound of breaking waves. There is no swelling and breaking in the undertow, no foam, no splash, no sound. Yet it is a powerful current and may move in a direction opposite to that of the waves, may move toward the open sea while they move toward the shore . . . To live in accord with the deeper rhythm might be to ignore the surface rhythm of life. It might mean missing the normal joys and cares of childhood, youth, manhood, and age. It might mean plunging down into the depths of life to follow a light as elusive as sea fire.[4]

Dunne's insight is applicable much more extensively than to the life of ministerial priesthood, but his image of a deeper life as an undertow which may run against the prevailing tide – you notice that it does not do so necessarily – which does not swell or break, which is unseen, because there is no foam, no splash, no sound, and which may involve sacrificing much that others regard as normal, speaks to me powerfully of the life which those who have been ordained embrace. It is an image we should take to heart.

4. John Dunne, *Time and Myth*, quoted in M. Basil Pennington OCSO, *Centering Prayer* (New York, 2001), pp. 160–1.

2

Jesus, Master and Friend

(i)

AT a turning-point in his ministry, when Jesus had reached the district of Caesarea Philippi, he raised a question with his disciples which has become famous. He asked them, 'Who do people say that I am?' And they gave him various answers. Then he pressed them personally, 'But who do you say I am?' (Mark 8:27–9 New Revised Standard Version; Matthew 16:13–15; Luke 9:18–19). It is a personal question for every Christian, but it has particular significance for those of us who are ordained. Whatever the reality of our lives, however inadequate we may feel we are, however far short of our own hopes we seem to ourselves to fall, the answer we give reveals at least the kind of priest we would like to be. How do we see Jesus? Who do we say that he is?

After leaving Oxford in the summer of 1989, I was able to have a sabbatical for six months. I had never had one before and was looking forward to it. Friends warned me that the time needed to be protected, because it would pass very quickly. So when someone telephoned me and asked me to join a pilgrimage to Israel that November as chaplain, I refused. I wanted to safeguard the sabbatical; that was my main reason, but also, like many others I know, because I had my own impressions of the Gospel scenes, I did not want them disturbed. But my refusal was not accepted. And in the course of further conversations I came to the view that, after almost twenty years as a priest, it was an opportunity not to be missed.

I have many memories of those days, but the most startling was on the Sea of Galilee. Like many pilgrim groups, our idea was to cross the lake on a small boat and pause in the middle, cutting the engine, reading an appropriate piece of Scripture, and spending some time in silence. Pilgrims to the Galilee will be familiar with the plan. But, as it happened, no small boat was available, which was a great disappointment. Instead we had to cross on a general passenger ferry where the atmosphere was hardly conducive to reflection. It was filled with tourists simply enjoying a day out. Many of them, I remember, were French, chatting happily and noisily. I imply no criticism. It was impossible to gather our group together. We were scattered. Then, at one point, I managed to climb a ladder and stand between decks to look out at the view. I was in a crowd, but alone. For all the modern development, I suddenly became aware of the water and was struck by how little the shape, the outline, the silhouette of the surrounding hills could have changed in two thousand years. What I was looking at was essentially a scene familiar to Jesus himself. I was intensely moved. It was a privileged moment. I was filled with a sense of his presence. Such an experience cannot be commanded. Not everyone can have my good fortune and pay such a visit to Israel. Those who do, will not necessarily feel as I felt. I have been several times since and crossed the lake in the smaller boat as originally planned on that occasion. I have valued those opportunities as well; they have been more obviously in tune with religious experience; but they cannot compare with that first time when, contrary to all reasonable expectation, in the midst of secular hubbub, for me the Lord was there.

'Who do *you* say that I am?' The question is powerful and important. What picture of Jesus do we have? Different people will answer in different ways. No one response can exhaust all the possibilities. However, let me offer some suggestions which I have found helpful and which may, therefore, be useful to others who want to explore the question for themselves.

One consequence of that visit to Israel was to make me take that question more seriously than ever. Church documents, like the Apostolic Exhortation on priestly formation, *Pastores Dabo Vobis* in 1992, tell me that as a priest I must be 'configured to Jesus Christ' (*Pastores Dabo Vobis*, n. 21). 'Configured' is an ungainly, abstract word. It means to be fashioned after a model. Jesus offers me a model, a pattern, an example I am to follow. So who is he? I am told that by virtue of my ordination, my spiritual life 'is marked, moulded and characterized by the way of thinking and acting proper to Jesus' (*Pastores Dabo Vobis*, n. 21). That is a compelling declaration. If my way of life is to be marked, moulded, and characterized by the way Jesus thinks and acts, I must come to know him intimately. How else can I measure up to what is expected of me? That pilgrimage taught me, first of all, that I must be aware of the context. Jesus was a Galilean and the Galilee is a revelation.

(ii)

Galilee is dominated by the lake which is the great source of water for the entire region. Today the issue of water rights is one of the controversial areas of dispute between Jews and Arabs. Water brings prosperity. That was as true two thousand years ago as it is now. It is unsurprising that Jesus' first disciples, Simon and Andrew, James and John, should have been fishermen. The Sea of Galilee supplied them and many others with their livelihood. And this expanse of water was not only a benefit for fishermen. It made it possible to irrigate the surrounding countryside as well. So the crops of farmers, especially the olive trees, could grow and shepherds had good grazing ground for their sheep and goats. This was a prosperous region. It was also isolated.

Look at a map of the time and you see to the west and north Phoenicia with the Gentile towns of Tyre and Sidon, to the east the Tetrarchy of Philip and, a little further south, the Decapolis region, ten towns with their largely Greek population, and then, completing the circle around Galilee, Samaria. So Galilee was an island, not enclosed by water, but by Gentiles and Samaritans.

The combination of prosperity and isolation has consequences. Most predictably, they breed self-confidence and forcefulness. The Galileans, relatively well off but separated from other Jews, had just that reputation. They were full of themselves and unabashed. They were also regarded as quarrelsome and aggressive. That was their style. By contrast, the Jews who were settled in cosmopolitan Jerusalem and who had appeased and accommodated the Roman occupier, looked on these northerners with contempt. They thought them stupid. During Jesus' ministry that contempt is illustrated by the incredulity, when Jesus becomes noticed, which mocks the idea that a prophet could come from Galilee and during his trial it is implied when Peter is identified by his accent (see John 7:41, 52, and Matthew 26:73). And they regarded the Galileans with suspicion as well. Insurrection came from the north: Galileans were seen as troublemakers; they were renowned for being extreme nationalists and rebellious.

This sketch is slight and simple, but it serves a useful purpose, as we try to see who Jesus was. It puts him in a context, economic, geographical, social, and political. When Jesus began his ministry, he did not arrive, so to speak, on an empty stage; he moved into a situation which was already in place. He had to handle people's preconceptions and prejudices. Seen against this backcloth, it is hardly surprising that when this charismatic preacher and healer emerged from the north, calling people to repentance and proclaiming the coming of the kingdom, he was going to meet resistance. The wonder of his message could easily be lost. Even with good will, the scope for misunderstanding was considerable. Whatever the truth of the matter, many people, especially those who felt threatened by his call to conversion, could argue that he was just another thick-headed Galilean troublemaker, gathering crowds of followers, who was intent on no-good and who would simply disturb the established order which they had managed to put in place with painstaking care. He had to be stopped.

Acknowledging the context also serves a deeper, more theological purpose. When he pressed the disciples with that personal question, 'Who do you say I am?', Peter answered, 'The Christ of God.' This reply, we know, is not an affirmation of Jesus' divinity, but nevertheless, when we hear it, it can be easy for us to slip lazily into familiar dogmatic formulae. Jesus is truly God and truly man: that is our unswerving faith. But such formulae serve a different purpose and in any case took centuries to compose. To find Jesus straining to make his message known in the midst of the complexities of his own society reminds us that the incarnation does not offer us cheap answers. Who do we say that he is? What picture of him do we have? Speaking personally, I would begin my own answer by turning to the opening of St Mark's Gospel.

(iii)

At the beginning, Jesus is baptized by John, spends forty days in the wilderness, begins to proclaim his message, calls his first four disciples, the fishermen, Simon and Andrew, James and John, visits the synagogue at Capernaum to preach and heal, spends the evening at Simon's house, and the following day, after praying in solitude, heals a leper. That summarizes the events. But when we read the passage – a mere thirty-five verses from the first chapter – we find running through it like a refrain the expression καὶ εὐθὺς, which is commonly translated 'and immediately'. It occurs eleven times. And so, Jesus was baptized and came up out of the water, *and immediately* he saw the Spirit descending on him; *and immediately* the Spirit drove him out into the wilderness; and on his return he called Simon and Andrew, *and immediately* they followed him; and he saw James and John, *and immediately* he called them and they followed him. He went to Capernaum *and immediately* on the Sabbath day he entered the synagogue and taught; *and immediately* a man with an unclean spirit called out at him and Jesus cured him; *and immediately* his fame spread everywhere. *And immediately* he left the synagogue and went to Simon's house where Simon's mother-in-law was sick *and immediately* he cured her. The following day a leper approached him, asking to be made clean, and Jesus touched him out of pity *and immediately* the leper was cleansed, *and immediately* he sent him away, ordering him to say nothing to anyone, but to go and show himself to the priest, as the Law required (see Mark 1:9–44).

The repetition has to be deliberate and, once noticed, it transforms the passage. It is a powerful enough account of the start of Jesus' ministry in any case, the baptism, the manifestation of the Spirit, the time in the wilderness, the calling of the first disciples, the early preaching and healing. But that phrase injects a quality into the events, an intensity and a dynamism. There is no other passage like it elsewhere in the Gospels, but it sets a tone. It is not a summons to the impossible ideal of perpetual availability, but rather it implies an energy and a sense of urgency. Here is a master who knows what he is about, someone to follow gladly and with confidence. But there is more to Jesus than his tirelessness during that early period around Capernaum.

(iv)

Mention of Capernaum stirs another memory. One day our pilgrim group was walking into the town. Our guide, Dudu Grinker, was striding ahead and I was bringing up the rear. Dudu is very tall and bearded, an instinctive teacher, imaginative, authoritative, and blessed with the soul of a poet. Suddenly he stopped and turned and called out to me, 'Father, come here.' I obeyed. As I reached him, he stretched up and plucked a pod from the tree overhead. 'Hold out your hand,' he commanded. I held it out. He shook his fist, cracked the pod, and two tiny dots rolled into my palm. 'What are those?' he asked. My mind was a blank. 'Those', he explained, 'are mustard seeds. If you come here in the right season, you will find this countryside covered with mustard trees.' It made me think of the disciples pestering Jesus. 'Come on,' they must have said to him, 'you are always talking about the kingdom. You began your ministry by proclaiming that the kingdom was close at hand. But what do you mean by the kingdom? Explain it to us.' And I imagined Jesus pausing and looking round and then, like Dudu, stretching up and doing to one of them what he had done to me, cracking a pod and releasing a seed into an outstretched palm, and saying, 'The kingdom of heaven is like a grain of mustard seed which a man took and sowed in his field; it is the smallest of all seeds, but when it has grown it is the greatest of shrubs and becomes a tree, so that the birds of the air come and make nests in its branches' (Matthew 13:31–2). Jesus taught by making connections with what they already understood. He built on their experience.

At the heart of St Matthew's Gospel is a discourse about the kingdom of heaven. We are told that Jesus explained many things in parables, but at this point all these parables are about the kingdom. One parable says that the kingdom of heaven is like a merchant in search of fine pearls who, when he finds one of great value, sells everything else he has in order to buy it. It is not necessarily the case, but for the sake of argument let's assume that the merchant was based in the city. All the other parables, however, are rural: the sower who goes out to sow, and some seed falls along the path, some on rocky ground, some in thorns, and some in good soil; the man who sowed good seed in his field, but an enemy came and sowed weeds; the mustard seed; the leaven which a woman took and hid in three measures of meal, till it was all leavened; the treasure hidden in a field; then – perhaps the exception –the merchant and the pearl; and finally, as the imagery shifts to the lake, the net cast into the sea which gathers in fish of every kind which then must be sorted, the good from the bad (see Matthew 13:1–52). Wander through Galilee. Contemplate the countryside. Gaze out over the lake. Jesus is not being obscure. He is teaching people by referring them to what they already knew and using it as a key to unlock fresh and deeper understanding.

Jesus is truly a teacher; he is not simply a teller. The method reveals the man. That fact was made clear to me during an afternoon some years ago, when a group of catechists, teachers, and priests from the Shrewsbury Diocese had gathered and David Wells, who is now working for the Diocese of Plymouth, helped us explore Jesus' method, *the way* he taught. It was unforgettable and I acknowledge very readily my debt to David in what follows next. As we come to see how Jesus worked, we are able to understand better the kind of person he was.

(v)

First of all, Jesus always respected the people who came to him. Sometimes that is illustrated by his use of questions. When he was approached by James and John, for example, and shortly afterwards by the blind beggar, Bartimaeus, he did not ask starkly, 'What do you want?', concerned only with the request, but 'What do you want me to do for you?' He was concerned about them as people, as individuals. The sons of Zebedee were being brash, while Bartimaeus was humble; the two occasions were very different,[1] but the question was the same: it was personal, addressing them, their needs, their desires (see Mark 10:36, 51).

This care for others is shown not only by the use of questions. It is also indicated by the way he never forced his viewpoint on others. Remember how he treated the rich young man whom we are told he looked at and loved. But this man, who wished to be perfect, could not accept the advice he received to go and sell everything he owned and become a follower of Jesus. It was not in fact an absolute command. A little earlier, a man who had been possessed, but whom Jesus had cured, had in fact wanted to leave everything and follow him, but Jesus prevented him. He told him to return to his friends instead and let them know what had been done for him. We don't all follow in the same way. Jesus' words to the rich man were a test. And he failed it. However, Jesus did not run after him and unravel the misunderstanding. He allowed him to make his own decision and respected it (see Mark 10:17–22; 5:1–20).[2] And there is a similar situation after Jesus' discourse on the bread of life. There

1. See Roderick Strange, *Living Catholicism* (London, 2001), pp. 87–91.
2. See *ibid.*, pp. 84–5.

were disciples then who said, 'This is a hard saying; who can listen to it?' And we are told that 'After this many of his disciples drew back and no longer went about with him' (John 6:60, 66). On this occasion too he respected them. He did not chase after them to try to counter their failure to understand him.

On other occasions Jesus made use of a particular situation to try to drive a lesson home. Here too questions could be helpful. So, after a day's teaching, he left the crowds and crossed the lake with his disciples in a boat. He fell asleep. There was a storm and waves washed into the boat and it began to fill. The disciples became alarmed and woke him. We are told that Jesus calmed the storm, but then turned to his companions and questioned them. 'Why are you afraid?' he asked. 'Have you no faith?' He is using the crisis as an opportunity. By examining the reason for their fear, they were being helped to consider the quality of their faith (see Mark 4:36–40; Matthew 8:23–6; Luke 8:22–5).

Then the parable of the labourers in the vineyard ended with questions as well. The men who had worked all day grumbled because those who were employed at the end of the day and had worked for only an hour, were paid the same full day's wage that they had received themselves. The householder in the parable does not explain. He asks one of them questions instead: 'Friend, I am doing you no wrong; did you not agree with me for a denarius? . . . Am I not allowed to do what I choose with what belongs to me? Or do you begrudge my generosity?' Here the questions serve a different purpose. The good teacher is so much more than a teller. Jesus asked these questions to help people work out their problems for themselves (see Matthew 20:1–15).

And in other circumstances we find him encouraging people to take responsibility for themselves. An outstanding example is the feeding of the five thousand in the Synoptic Gospels. Jesus has taken the disciples apart to a quiet, lonely place, where they can be alone, but the people guess where they are going and so, when they arrive, they find a crowd gathered. Jesus talks to them at length, but, as evening draws in, the disciples suggest that he send the people away to find something to eat before they return home. But he says, 'You give them something to eat' (Mark 6:37; see Matthew 14:16; Luke 9:13). We cannot be expected to perform a miracle like that, but his reaction to the disciples' request to send the people away, however worthy their motives, is a reminder to us, especially as priests, that, when people turn to us in need, we must not avoid our responsibilities.

When we explore the way Jesus taught, we find that these elements – his respect for people, his use of a situation as an opportunity, his gift for helping people solve their problems for themselves, and his encouragement to them to take responsibility – come together in St Luke's Gospel in the passage which culminates in the parable of the Good Samaritan. It may help to recall the context.

There was a standard question put to rabbis: what is the first of all the commandments? It was put to Jesus in each of the Synoptic Gospels, and, as we know, he would reply with the *Shema Israel* (see Deuteronomy 6:4–5), but in each Gospel the context changes: in Matthew it is part of a series of questions through which his critics hoped to trap him (see Matthew 22:34–40); in Mark a scribe whom Jesus will praise as 'not far from the kingdom of God', approaches him (see Mark 12:28–34); and in Luke a lawyer tries to test him. This Lucan account is particularly instructive.

Once again, questions are in play. First of all, there is the question put to Jesus. The lawyer asked, 'Teacher, what shall I do to inherit eternal life?' Jesus did not tell him, but replied by inviting him to give his own view: 'What is written in the law? How do you read?' And so on this occasion it was the man who spoke, uttering the *Shema Israel*: 'You shall love the Lord your God with all your heart, and with all your soul, and with all your strength, and with all your mind: and your neighbour as yourself.' By asking questions Jesus had drawn the answer from the man and he acknowledged what he had said: 'You have answered right; do this and you shall live.' But the lawyer was not satisfied and pressed Jesus with a further question. He asked him, 'And who is my neighbour?' Still Jesus did not give him a direct answer. Instead he told him the parable of the Good Samaritan, about the man who fell among thieves and was ignored by the priest and the Levite, but was helped by the Samaritan. He made his teaching come alive for the man by using his prejudice against Samaritans: Jews despised Samaritans; it was inconceivable for him that the neighbour whom he should love as himself, could be the Samaritan. But Jesus pressed him with a final question: 'Which of these three, do you think, proved neighbour to the man who fell among the robbers?' The lawyer, for all that he was trying to test Jesus, was treated throughout with respect. The answer may be inescapable, but he had to give it himself. He had to take responsibility for it. It stuck in his throat and he could not bring himself to name the Samaritan, so he replied, 'The one who showed mercy on him.' And he was instructed to go and do likewise (see Luke 10:25–37).

This parable illustrates briefly and simply how Jesus worked with people when he taught them, respecting them, using the opportunity as it arose, but helping them to discover the truth for themselves and take responsibility for it. As we come to notice how he worked, so we may see more clearly the kind of person he was, the kind of person in a particular way a priest is called to be. It is time to weave some of the threads together.

(vi)

Although Jesus was divine, when he was born, he did not walk on to an empty stage. Like every other human being, he inherited a given situation, the history, the politics, the economics, the conflicts, the prejudices of his time. He had to deal with that, the good and the bad, the strengths and the weaknesses, the joys and the sorrows. We all do. It is no different within priesthood. We are not born into, or ordained into, a perfect world. We have to grasp our opportunities and face up to our limitations, giving thanks for the blessings we have received and confronting the scandals. If we are to be effective priests, there is no alternative.

If our approach to our ministry, then, is to be inspired by his, it may be that the opening passage of St Mark's Gospel with its sense of tireless energy can set the tone. I'm not suggesting that we have to become slaves to relentless, mindless, exhausting activity, but that we are called to an utterly unselfish commitment to the service of others. We are to give and not to count the cost. And teaching is central.

Priests are always teachers. Because I went to a Jesuit school, I have often been asked why, when I decided to become a priest, I did not choose to become a Jesuit, and my stock reply has been, 'Because I didn't want to be a teacher.' I meant, of course, a classroom teacher, but I have long been aware of the irony: I have been involved with education and teaching throughout my priestly life. All priests are. And Jesus is our model.

He set himself to teach people. And his methods should shape ours. As we preach from the pulpit, as we counsel individuals, as we work with various groups, whether adults preparing for baptism or reception into the Church, or children preparing to receive sacraments, or their parents, whoever it may be and whatever the situation, we try to follow his example. He treated people with respect. It showed itself in his awareness of their circumstances and their needs. Consider a contrast. A friend of mine took a group on a tour to Florence to see the great art treasures of that city. For two days the guide assigned to them was one of the most learned of all, but she spoke at great length and was far too detailed, oblivious to the tiredness which was gradually overwhelming her audience. Jesus, on the other hand, as we have seen, was sensitive to people; he built on their experience and used what they already knew, rural images, for example, or the conflict between Jews and Samaritans, to help them understand more. He asked them questions, took advantage of opportunities which occurred, even a storm on the lake, and helped them take responsibility for what they were learning. He was a good teacher. He formed relationships with those who came to see him; he was not just a teller, a supplier of answers.

As we appreciate his qualities and his way of working, Jesus of Nazareth comes alive for us. We must try to acquire the same skills and become like him, the kind of person he was. We too must respect those we serve, build on what they already know, and help them to learn by reflecting on their experiences. We must use situations imaginatively and encourage people to take responsibility for their faith.

(vii)

When Jesus began his ministry, we are told that he impressed those who heard him because he taught them with authority. It is stated twice, for example, in that passage at the beginning of St Mark's Gospel which we considered earlier (see Mark 1:22, 27). But there is development. At first, when Jesus called people to him, he was the master and they in a sense were the servants. But by the end of his ministry the disciples were servants no longer. In his words to them at the Last Supper in St John's Gospel, he told them, 'No longer do I call you servants, for the servant does not know what his master is doing; but I have called you friends, for all that I have heard from my Father I have made known to you' (15:15). Jesus the master has become the friend. The disciples are no longer simply being instructed. As friends they are to be allies in his mission. But the matter doesn't end there. It may sound wonderful to be the friend of Jesus, but friends must face the consequences. We need to return to the Sea of Galilee.

You will remember the scene at the end of the Fourth Gospel when Jesus, risen from the dead, confronts Peter on the shore of the lake and asks him a question – again he uses questions. In fact, he asks him the same question three times: 'Simon, son of John, do you love me?' And Peter's repeated declaration of love is seen as cancelling his triple denial during Jesus' passion. Jesus accepts his word and once again gives him responsibilities,

'Feed my lambs . . . feed my sheep.' The passage is significant for an understanding of the Petrine ministry (John 21:15–19). But it may have something more personal to teach us as well.

The questions don't need to be read as addressed only to Peter. As priests, how do we hear them addressed to us? I was once given this passage as a prompt for prayer as a penance after I had been to confession, and it suddenly burst into life for me.

I heard the question the first time, 'Do you love me?' 'Yes, Lord, you know that I love you.' 'Be a good priest.' I heard it again, not more insistent, quiet and calm as before, 'Do you love me?' 'Yes, Lord, you know that I love you.' 'Be a faithful priest.' Then I heard it for the third time: the tone of voice hadn't changed, it was still calm and patient, 'Do you love me?' And like Peter I was moved. I knew I had been heard and yet I was still being asked. And like Peter I replied, 'Lord, you know everything. You know that I love you.' 'Be a good priest.' We too are summoned to love and in our own way are given responsibilities to be good shepherds, feeding the lambs and sheep.

To hear the question repeated and to reply to it is to find our resolve strengthened. But there is something more. This is not an exercise in sentimental piety. We hear next a further line, because Jesus goes on, 'Truly, truly, I say to you, when you were young, you girded yourself and walked where you would; but when you are old, you will stretch out your hands, and another will gird you and carry you where you do not wish to go' (John 21:18). The immediate reference is a prophecy of Peter's death, but for us too it has significance.

A priest does not have control over his own life. We cannot be priests on our own terms, simply doing what suits us. In the stark words of Pope John Paul II, 'Priests are not there to serve themselves, but the People of God' (*Pastores Dabo Vobis*, n. 78). Demands will be made of us which may go against the grain and which test our courage. We follow a crucified Lord and are asked to respond generously. The implications may be costly. We have met one image for that already. A priest's life, lived at depth, is like the undertow. It is not foam and splash and sound, but something that may move against the prevailing tide or run along the shore. It doesn't simply rush to the beach like the surf. And the time may come when faithful service means that we have to hold out our hands and be led where we would rather not go. Discipleship is a risky business. We must be ready to run that risk.

3

Risking the Cross

(i)

To speak of ministerial priesthood in terms of risk may seem to some at best inappropriate, at worst a contradiction. We are taught that those who are ordained are called to model themselves on Jesus, to shape their lives as he had shaped his. But how, it may be asked, can that discipleship entail risk? What risk did Jesus run? What risk could he run? Truly human, he was none the less truly divine. The Word became flesh to save us from our sins. He would suffer and die and triumph. He knew that. The conclusion was never in doubt. He endured torture and brutal execution, but he ran no risks. He knew the outcome. He knew he would be raised. And so, the argument might continue, to speak of our discipleship, the way we follow him, as entailing risk is misconceived. He risked nothing. Configured to him, neither do we. The path of discipleship is assured, not free from suffering, but free from risk.

Perhaps, however, we should step back and review the situation. Jesus saved us from our sins by dying on the cross. It is a statement we repeat often, but it deserves a closer look. What more precisely was the part played by the cross in our salvation? We know we are not saved by any cross. We are not saved by the cross of Spartacus or by the crosses of the thieves who were crucified with Jesus. It is not any crucifixion that will do. We are saved by the cross of Jesus, by that cross alone. What makes his cross special? It had a context. What did Jesus come for?

(ii)

The Gospels indicate that Jesus foresaw what would happen to him. He foretold his passion. But he did not come to die. We are so used to saying that he did that these words can shock us. They appear scandalous. But they are not. They unveil for us the mystery and the meaning of the cross more clearly.

Jesus came not to die, but to love. He came to reconcile us to the Father by making the Father's love known. That was his mission. Although we were created by God out of love, when we sinned, we rejected that love and separated ourselves from God. Jesus came to restore that relationship of love. He came to reveal to us through his preaching and by his very person that the Father loves us without reserve. We may have separated ourselves from the Father, but the Father has never abandoned us. Jesus was committed completely to making that love known; he wanted it to overwhelm us; he wanted us to find it irresistible. He did not want the good news of this love to be rejected. He wanted it to be welcomed. How could he have wished for anything else? So he did not come to die, but to do his Father's will. That was his vocation. He gave himself totally to this ministry, and so he accepted its consequences, whatever they might be, whatever the cost, whatever the outcome, whatever the sufferings he had to endure, even death, death on a cross, to win us back. There was nothing he would not do.

His passion and death appal us. He was scourged and crowned with thorns, slapped and spat upon, fastened to the cross and left to hang there. His physical condition will have fulfilled the prophecy of Isaiah: he was 'one from whom men hide their faces' (Isaiah 53:3). Crucifixion, in Herbert McCabe's phrase, 'was essentially death by public helplessness'.[1] It is a telling description. Although at one level Jesus had foreseen the outcome of his mission, at another in his passion he had been handed over, he had lost control. He was passive, not active. He

1. Herbert McCabe, *God Matters* (London, 1987), p. 97.

was at the mercy of events. He was helpless. He sacrificed himself, laid down his life, so that, when everything else seemed to have failed, his suffering and agonized death would still make plain his unfailing love: 'Greater love has no man than this, that a man lay down his life for his friends' (John 15:14); 'God shows his love for us in that while we were yet sinners Christ died for us' (Romans 5:8).

There is a fine balance here. Jesus did not die deliberately, but nor did he die by chance. His death on the cross was not a careless accident. He could see what would happen, but he did not simply choose to suffer. In this sense, to use the language at the heart of these reflections, the cross was not his initiative. It was not a risk of his choosing, but rather the consequence of his commitment. In that sense his mission involved the risk of discipleship. His sufferings and crucifixion were the supreme sign of that risk. Here we find the true meaning of the cross: it is planted at the heart of our faith, not as a predetermined strategy, but as the undeniable sign of the limitless love which calls us home. It was not inevitable. In principle, people might have welcomed the good news Jesus proclaimed. In fact they did not. And so Jesus accepted the consequences of his mission so as to make possible our salvation. He risked the cross for our sake. He ran the risk of discipleship.

All the baptized are called to share that risk, to accept the consequences of their commitment. But those who have been ordained have a particular responsibility to set an example. We knowingly place ourselves at risk. We must accept the consequences of our ordination, come what may. What form may that risk take?

(iii)

Most of us will not be required to suffer spectacularly or publicly. Our sufferings, the risks we have to endure, are more likely to be less obvious, but they may be none the less severe for that. We may not foresee them. They may take us by surprise. The pain will lie in the unpredictability. That is how we will share the cross of Christ. The unpredictable is beyond our control. Like Jesus we will be helpless, at the mercy of events. Will we still drink the cup and be baptized with his baptism? Will we accept the risk of discipleship? Where might we find it? Let us return to the rich young man. His meeting with Jesus has often been used to explain the nature of vocation to the priesthood or the religious life as a higher calling. But, I suggest, that misses the point. It blunts the challenge. The lesson is more subtle and alarming.

Remember the scene. This young man has approached Jesus, motivated by a high ideal. He wants to know what good deed he must do if he is to have eternal life. Jesus advises him to keep the commandments, not to kill, steal, commit adultery, and the rest. He can give a good account of himself. 'All these I have observed;' he replies, 'what do I still lack?' St Mark tells us that Jesus looked at him and loved him, so the man was presumably telling the truth; he was a good man. Then Jesus says to him, 'If you would be perfect, go, sell what you possess and give to the poor, and you will have treasure in heaven; and come follow me' (Matthew 19:16–22; see Mark 10:21). But he goes away sorrowful because he cannot give up his riches.

What conclusions can we draw? First, we should recognize that the perfection he was being offered is not something absolute, as though those who have property and wealth are inescapably less perfect than those who do not. As we have noticed already, the invitation to go and sell, come and follow, is personal and particular, a test for him, not for all.[2] We don't all need to go and sell everything we possess to qualify as disciples. Second, however, he was being sifted. Jesus was challenging him at the point where he was most vulnerable. There was a lesson he needed to learn. How genuine and deep was his desire for eternal life? It was not as deep and genuine as he had imagined. Jesus invited him to follow a path, but he found it too

2. See above, p. 16.

costly. He could not bring himself to accept the consequences of the invitation he was being offered.

I like to think that the young man went away sorrowful, not because his wish had been thwarted, but because he had learnt something about himself. He had discovered his weakness. Jesus does that. When he puts us to the test, he reveals to us our true priorities. 'Where your treasure is, there will your heart be also' (Matthew 6:21). Although he had not been aware of it before, the rich young man's treasure was where his treasure was and his heart was with it. He could not bring himself to put it at risk. However deep his desire for perfection and eternal life, the desire was qualified. And there is a lesson here for us as well. When we are invited to accept ministerial priesthood, we too are being challenged at the point where we are most vulnerable. We are being invited to run the risk of discipleship. We must accept the consequences completely, whatever they may be.

So where is our treasure? Where is our heart? What matters most to us? The Lord will search it out. He will expose it. We say we want to be his disciples. Are we prepared to run the risk of discipleship? What will we risk for Christ's sake? How much will we risk? The cross we will be asked to carry may be something we find unbearable, something from which we want to find relief at any cost, but we are invited to carry it nevertheless, to die a death by helplessness.

What form will the risk of discipleship take? What lesson can we learn from the experience of the rich young man? We learn that it will challenge us to the very core of our being, reveal to us where we are most vulnerable. The demand may seem to be insupportable. Left to ourselves, it is. We may decide that it is impossible, but the question, as Jesus explained to the disciples when they were reflecting on the young man's visit, is not what is possible for us, but what is possible for God. He can lead a camel through the eye of a needle. He can enable us to accept and run the risk of discipleship. That is the form it takes within our hearts. The risk is personal and utterly profound.

(iv)

But the risk of discipleship is not only interior. What touches our very depths will show itself outwardly as well. The risk of discipleship can take many forms. Some may attract public attention, while others pass virtually unnoticed. The risk involved may be no less demanding.

The point is illustrated by the contrasting experiences of two great archbishops. The story of Oscar Romero is well known. He was a reserved, rather conservative kind of man, who, it was supposed, would keep affairs under calm control when he was appointed Archbishop of San Salvador. But the plight of the people in his care and the injustices to which they were subjected changed him. He spoke for those who could not speak for themselves. He became the voice of the voiceless. Brother bishops distanced themselves from him. He was isolated. I imagine he must often have been frightened. But his faith gave him the courage to master his fear. He remained steadfast and was shot dead while saying mass in 1980. He evidently accepted the consequences of his commitment, the risk of discipleship. And then, by contrast, there is the story of Helder Camara, who was Archbishop of Olinda and Recife in North-east Brazil. Here too was a hero of the faith who brought the gospel to the poor of his diocese by the power of his example. His ministry was outstanding. He was opposed and censored in his country. And so he travelled the world, preaching his vision of non-violence as the way to counter injustice. His fidelity put him at risk, but he was never shot. Instead, when he became seventy-five, his resignation was accepted promptly and for the remaining fourteen years of his life he had to watch his work being dismantled by his successor. He died in 1999. For him the outcome, the experience of risk, was very different.

Then, in more recent years, particularly in the United States, in Britain and Australia, the consequences of discipleship, the risk it involves, have taken another form. The suffering that has taken us more by surprise than anything we could ever have imagined, has been through the uncovering of scandals relating to the sexual abuse of children by some priests and religious. It has been a nightmare. Nothing is to be compared with the pain of those who have been abused. The discovery of this behaviour – serial abuse, boys lured into bed, children forced to perform oral sex – appals us. That children should ever be treated in that way is sickening. We grieve for the survivors and victims and ask for pardon. Trust is an indispensable part of any significant personal relationship. To betray trust is to wound and undermine a person's capacity for trust. It is an injury which will take years to heal. It can scar people for life. That priests should abuse their position of unquestioning trust to betray the innocent beggars belief.[3] And besides the harm they have done to the young, there is the damage they have inflicted on their brothers, on other priests and religious.

The guilty may indeed be few, but their actions have made all priests feel compromised. A calling which has filled us with joy and humble pride, has been tarnished by shame. A journalist has observed, 'The figure of the saintly, benign counsellor, a comforting presence in times of distress, a resolute ally in the face of danger, is giving way to a quite different image – a cunning and deceitful deviant.'[4] The stream of media reporting and comment damages morale. Much of it comes from the best of motives, but there are other agendas also in play. There are those who oppose the Church and are delighted to have a platform for their crusade, while men who for decades have indeed lived lives of utter probity, as counsellors and comforters and courageous allies in times of crisis, have found here a pain they could never have predicted, something beyond imagining. They grieve for the victims, are shamed by the guilty, and are mortified by the ineffective way these offences have too often been handled in the past. Their own behaviour has been beyond

3. See William J. Bausch, *Breaking Trust: a Priest Looks at the Scandal of Sexual Abuse* (Mystic, CT, 2002).
4. Nicholas Wapshott, 'How the neighbourhood priest was betrayed by lies and lust', *The Times*, 7 December 2002.

reproach, yet they are stigmatised as cunning and deceitful deviants. For those who also happen to be homosexual, the situation can be even worse. When wrong has been done, people look instinctively for someone to blame. In spite of their chastity, they may be used as scapegoats.

The cross can take many forms. We cannot predict the consequences of discipleship, the risks we may be asked to run. Is there any way we can be prepared? How can we brace ourselves for such risks and the pain of the unpredictable?

(v)

Consider a common situation. When we are ordained, we are full of ideals. We read St Paul's words to the Philippians and our hearts are set on fire. We make them our own: 'I believe nothing can happen that will outweigh the supreme advantage of knowing Christ Jesus my Lord. For him I have accepted the loss of everything and I look on everything as so much rubbish, if only I can have Christ and be given a place in him' (Philippians 3:8–9 Jerusalem Bible). We are filled with enthusiasm. We look forward to being appointed to parishes or given responsibilities where our gifts can flourish so that we can serve the gospel generously. And that may be our experience and all will seem well. We are happy and appear to others to be tireless in the work we do.

Then one day we find we are put to the test. We are given a new appointment, just as necessary, but less appealing. A time comes for most of us when our lesser gifts are called into play. It would be wonderful always to be a square peg in a square hole, but at some stage we will probably be asked to fit into a hole which is round. A friend of mine once described to me what it is like to be a square peg in a round hole. 'It means', he said, 'being in a position which plays to your weaknesses rather than your strengths.' I find that explanation illuminating because it takes us to the heart of discipleship. It suggests at once consequences beyond our control, the risks which are not of our choosing.

When given responsibilities, we like to feel we can carry them out. We don't want to feel incapable or inadequate. That is natural enough. The situation is testing. When we lack confidence, we feel insecure and vulnerable. Almost by definition we are less sure of our lesser gifts. In these circumstances, how do we react? We may feel threatened, at risk. Here indeed we may find our cross, the pain we had not been able to predict, the suffering which takes us by surprise. Our instinct may well be to act on our own terms, so as to retain control and avoid the risk. We argue that we need to feel confidence in our ability to do what has been asked of us. How else, we may ask, can we be effective?

But is that what we really think? And if we do, what is it revealing to us of our own understanding of the ministry we exercise? Are we just being priests on our own terms? Or do we believe in fact that 'the foolishness of God is wiser than men, and the weakness of God is stronger than men'? Do we believe that 'God chose what is foolish in the world to shame the wise, God chose what is weak in the world to shame the strong' (1 Corinthians 1:25, 27)? Do I believe that 'when I am weak, then I am strong' (2 Corinthians 12:10)?

If I always consult my own convenience, if I will play only to my strengths, refusing work with which I do not feel at ease, what I do can always be seen as my own achievement. How then can God's glory be revealed in me? My priesthood is shown up as something based on my terms, not his. I am giving, but counting the cost, calculating the risk. I should not seek responsibilities when I know I am incompetent: that would be absurd and irresponsible. But I must be ready at times to be a square peg in a round hole, to risk being in a position which plays to my weaknesses rather than my strengths, which makes use of my lesser gifts, instead of my greater ones. I must prepare myself for that. Then I will be led where I would rather not go. I will have to follow the undertow rather than the surf. I must trust. I have to be ready to abandon myself and take up the cross. The cross is the place where Jesus revealed his total self-abandonment to the Father: 'into thy hands I commit my spirit' (Luke 23:46). He accepted the consequences of his mission. And I too must be ready to accept the risks of discipleship, whatever they may be.

When we find we are despised as irrelevant, deceitful, and hypocritical, we must face that attitude courageously. Our discipleship needs to be disciplined, if we are to follow the undertow and be led where we would rather not go. We follow the path of sacrifice and risk the cross. We must be clear that dedicated discipleship will involve risk. We prepare ourselves for that. It is no good waiting till the time of crisis arrives. We must look ahead. We must develop deliberately a disposition for responding to that risk. What kind of disposition will that be? One image more recently has helped me.

(vi)

When Jesus sent the twelve out on mission, he told them, 'be wise as serpents and innocent as doves' (Matthew 10:16). It is a difficult saying, but not long ago I read with fresh eyes the interpretation offered by St John Chrysostom.

We normally think of the serpent as wily rather than wise, but it is wise, Chrysostom says, in one sense: it will slough off its skin, it is ready to abandon everything, even its own body, provided only it can save its head. In the same way, he teaches, our commitment means we must abandon everything except our faith; we must be ready to give up our wealth, our body, and life itself. The serpent then is a symbol of total commitment, a symbol of those who will risk all for what they value most. It is not, however, a symbol of the way risk is to be taken. The serpent is associated with cunning and deceit. So how is the risk to be taken? Not with the serpent's cunning or with violence, nor, we may add, in a deceitful, manipulative, self-protective way. There is no place here for self-interest or saving face. This wisdom, Chrysostom goes on, is no use without innocence. Wisdom and innocence must be partners, and he identifies innocence with the dove, a bird which refuses to take vengeance on those who do it harm.[5] The image of the serpent and the dove, the alliance between wisdom and innocence, can show us how to run the risk of discipleship.

Day by day we try to strengthen our sense of commitment: what do we value most, where is our treasure, where is our heart? What stirs us to risk everything? If it is discipleship, if our treasure is found in Christ, then his sacrifice guides us. He abandoned everything in fidelity to his Father's will and out of love for us. And we must put the service of the gospel before everything else and cultivate innocence, gentleness, and generosity. Jesus refused to retaliate against those who assaulted him; he 'became obedient unto death, even death on a cross' (Philippians 2:8). We practise following the same path. That was the lesson he came to teach us. In Hilary Davies's stark words,

> We are now at the very heartland, under
> The long crossed shadow of God showing how to die.[6]

Then, when we have learnt that lesson, whatever the risks may be, whatever form our cross-bearing may take – public or hidden, dramatic or long-drawn-out, foreseen or unimagined – we will hope to be faithful to the undertow, not the surf. We follow the way of wisdom and innocence. We remain faithful while we resign ourselves to being led where we do not wish to go. We risk all for our treasure, for the gospel, for Christ's sake. That is where our heart is. We suffer, but do not strike back. We follow his way. As Jesus abandoned himself without resentment to his death on the cross, so we, when put to the test, remain gently steadfast. We become one with him.

An outstanding contemporary example of this disposition is

5. See John Chrysostom, Homilies on St Matthew's Gospel, 33:2; Thirty-fourth Thursday of the Year, *The Divine Office.*
6. Hilary Davies, 'Stations of the Cross XII, Christ Dies upon the Cross', *In a Valley of This Restless Mind* (London, 1997), p. 23.

Fr Pedro Arrupe, who was the General of the Society of Jesus. He was the first Basque to be General of the Jesuits since their founder, Ignatius Loyola. He had spent long years working in Japan and had experienced the dropping of the Atom Bomb on Hiroshima in August 1945 and cared for the survivors. As General, he had guided Jesuits worldwide in the turbulent, heady days following the Second Vatican Council. It became a difficult time. The Pope intervened in the running of the Society. Arrupe suffered a stroke and, although elected for life, was finally allowed to resign from his office on the morning of 3 September 1983. That afternoon the General Congregation which had accepted his resignation, gathered to hear his message to the Society. It had to be read for him. His stroke had left him incapable of speech. He told them:

> More than ever I find myself in the hands of God. This is what I have wanted all my life from my youth. It is the one thing I continue to desire. But now there is a difference: today the initiative is entirely with the Lord. I assure you it is indeed a profound experience to know and feel myself to be completely in his hands.[7]

What extraordinary words from a sick and exhausted man, a victim of misunderstanding. How wonderful for us also to be able to say of our reliance on God: 'This is what I have wanted all my life from my youth. It is the one thing I continue to desire.'

It is never easy to run the risk of discipleship, to make a commitment and be ready to accept the consequences whatever they may be. There is a daily dying which needs to take place, a daily conversion. We try to become habitually generous. We

7. 'Yo me siento, mas que nunca, en las manos de Dios. Eso es lo que he deseado toda di mi vida, desde joven. Y eso tambien lo unico que sigo queriendo ahora. Pero con una diferencia: Hoy toda la iniciativa la tiene el Senor. Les aseguro que saberme y sentirme totalmente en sus manos es una profunda experiencia', *Acta Romana Societatis Iesu*, vol. 18, n. 4, 1983, 3 septembris 1983.

may seem to die within ourselves. Our hopes may be destroyed. We may feel desolate, abandoned, defeated. The risk is great. But, if we persevere, we find that we are changed, transformed. It is Christ's power and wisdom that will shine through, not our own. By accepting the risk of discipleship, we follow his way. We bind ourselves to him more closely and it may be said of us what Paul could claim for himself: 'I have been crucified with Christ; it is no longer I who live, but Christ who lives in me' (Galatians 2:20).

4

Priests and Presbyters

(i)

One of the most moving moments in a priest's ordination comes when the bishop addresses those who are to be ordained and instructs them, 'Imitate the mystery you celebrate.' It is an invitation 'to die to sin and to walk in the new life of Christ'. They are being asked to respond to the undertow rather than the surf, to be led where they would rather not go, to be square pegs in round holes. The invitation has always been there, but it has been understood differently at different times and its impact has sometimes become apparent only gradually. That's all right. Some people feel that the demands of this vocation can only be justified if they have always been known clearly from the beginning, and so at one extreme there are those who pour energy into demonstrating that Jesus ordained the Twelve at the Last Supper, while at the other there are those who argue that the character of ministry was much more obscure in the early Church and on that basis conclude that nothing was established definitively at all, it was simply a matter of administrative convenience. Neither position is satisfactory. The irony lies in the fact that these contrasting views share a conviction about the need for clarity of consciousness. The former uses it to establish a rigid position, while the latter is equally insistent about its importance, but claims that its absence gives grounds for complete freedom. It will not do. We need to start elsewhere.

When we consider ministerial priesthood in the Catholic Church through the course of the centuries, we find it lit by different emphases. Let me sketch the familiar story again to help us get it more clearly into perspective; but we must begin with the Scriptures.

(ii)

The first chapter of St Mark's Gospel ends with a limpid phrase. It states simply, 'people came to him from every quarter' (Mark 1:45). From the earliest time in his ministry, people gathered around Jesus. They came in large numbers. We are soon told that when he withdrew with his disciples, 'a great multitude from Galilee followed'. He went into the hills and there he 'called to him those whom he desired; and they came to him'. So from the crowds some were called specially; and then from these disciples, 'he appointed twelve, to be with him, and to be sent out to preach and have authority to cast out demons' (see Mark 3:7, 13–19). From early on, therefore, some were invited in a particular way 'to be with him'. There was a reason for it. They were commissioned to preach and to overcome evil. They were to assist Jesus in proclaiming the good news: 'The time is fulfilled, and the kingdom of God is at hand; repent, and believe in the gospel' (Mark 1:15). They had a part in that ministry. He sent them out, two by two (see Mark 6:7), and instructed them to preach that 'the kingdom of heaven is at hand' and to 'heal the sick, raise the dead, cleanse lepers, [and] cast out demons' (Matthew 10:7–8). Then, after Jesus had been raised from the dead, their work acquired fresh meaning. St Luke speaks of the risen Jesus opening his disciples' minds to understand the Scriptures and saying to them, 'Thus it is written, that the Christ should suffer and on the third day rise from the dead, and that repentance and forgiveness of sins should be preached in his name to all nations, beginning from Jerusalem. You are witnesses of these things' (Luke 24:47–8). They were sent out to preach.

Shortly before, on the night of his betrayal, Jesus had gathered with the Twelve for his last supper. We know the scene well. He took bread, gave thanks, broke the bread, and gave it to them. As he did so, he identified himself with the bread he handed them, saying, 'This is my body.' And similarly with the cup, which he took and for which he gave thanks, and they all drank, and Jesus said, 'This is my blood.' And he instructed them to do the same as a memorial of him, 'Do this in remembrance of me' (see 1 Corinthians 11:23–5; Matthew 26:26–8; Mark 14:22–4; Luke 22:19–20). They were to celebrate this thanksgiving, this eucharist, in his memory. And they did as they were asked. St Paul's account to the Corinthians is the earliest we have, written at most thirty years after the event and notable because it is evidence of well-established behaviour; Paul is not suggesting to them something new and unfamiliar.

However, as we know, the Fourth Gospel omits any account of the institution of the eucharist. In its place Jesus washes the disciples' feet and then explains what he has done: 'You call me Teacher and Lord; and you are right, for so I am. If I then, your Lord and Teacher, have washed your feet, you also ought to wash one another's feet. For I have given you an example, that you should also do as I have done to you' (John 13:13–15). They are to be humble servants, following the Lord's example. This washing of feet is a dramatic illustration. From the earliest stages of his ministry Jesus had associated with those who were despised, sinners, prostitutes, and tax collectors (see Mark 2:16), and he promised eternal life to those who fed the hungry and gave drink to the thirsty, who welcomed the homeless and clothed the naked, and who visited those who were sick or in prison (see Matthew 25:31–46). He identified himself with those in need. To serve them was to serve him.

All this is well known to us. We have touched on these points more briefly already. I mention them now because we see in these events different emphases. The preaching of the word, the celebration of sacraments, of which the eucharist is source and summit, and the service of those in need can always be discerned. They are the raw material for ministerial priesthood and at this stage it was very raw indeed. Clarity about its significance emerged gradually. At the time there was no clear awareness of it.

(iii)

The importance of preaching, of proclamation, was, however, clear from the start. And so, for example, when there was an early dispute between the Hebrews and the Hellenists over the daily distribution to widows, the Twelve appointed Stephen and six others to carry out that duty so that they themselves would remain free to preach (see Acts 6:1–6). Preaching was the priority. And the letters to Timothy and to Titus make the same point regularly and with great force. Timothy must 'attend to the public reading of scripture, to preaching, to teaching' (1 Timothy 4:13); he must preach 'in season and out of season' (2 Timothy 4:2); and Titus is urged to 'teach what befits sound doctrine' (Titus 2:1).

At the beginning, then, there was this desire to continue the public ministry of Jesus. Preaching and teaching, proclamation and prophecy took pride of place. But when the break with Judaism came and the Temple was destroyed, and as the community grew and spread and suffered persecution, another need was recognized and another element in ministry began to emerge. There had to be structures to support the charisms which were being exercised. Disputes soon arose as well. Whose teaching was authentic? So leaders had to be appointed to preserve the community's identity as the community of Christ. Even from the early days these leaders may have presided at the eucharist as well. Ignatius of Antioch taught that the only legitimate eucharist was one celebrated under the presidency of the bishop (see Ignatius, Letter to the Smyrnaeans, 8,1–2), but, if they did preside, it would have been because they were already leaders. They were not made leaders simply because they presided at the eucharist. Leadership, the care for the community, had become the new priority.

That remained true for centuries, through the early centuries of persecution and then the later, more settled years, following the conversion of Constantine, when Christianity became the established religion of the Roman Empire. During that whole period bishops emerged gradually as full and undisputed leaders, while in due course the presbyters, who at first had been esteemed for their mature faith rather than any ministerial function, came to form the bishop's Council and could be delegated to act for him. This was at last the time – during the fourth century – when the sacramental dimension developed more evidently and the presbyter came to be seen as the priest. He wore special clothes. There was the move from the functional understanding of his role to regarding it as a state of life. Someone who had been seen as the unifier of the community came to be recognized as a dispenser of grace. A distinction can be detected between clergy and laity.

When the Roman Empire collapsed, there was a period of confusion, marked by a struggle between the Pope, the Patriarch of Constantinople, and the Emperor of Byzantium. The influence of the papacy, however, grew, notably through the example of Pope Gregory the Great. Gregory, himself a monk, made extensive use of monks to evangelize. He sent Augustine to Britain. And this kind of initiative had two major consequences. First, ministry came to follow the monastic pattern and so became feudal, reflecting the hierarchical character of monastic life. And, second, as monasticism came to be more sacerdotal, ministry became identified as liturgy, so that to care for the Body of Christ now came to mean to care for the eucharistic species and not, as formerly, the Christian community. A further shift had taken place. Now the cultic, the sacramental ministry, became the priority and in time this view took an even firmer grip.

The battle fought and won by Pope Gregory VII, who died in 1085, to keep the secular power out of the sanctuary, led to a still narrower understanding of ministry. The emphasis was placed distinctly on the sacral and on the eucharist. Priesthood was seen as a power, the power to celebrate the eucharist, rather than a ministry of service. That was what was most important of all. And so episcopacy, as a consequence, was regarded indeed as a dignity and an office, but not as the fullness of priesthood.

It became a mere jurisdictional appendix to priestly power. The central purpose of priesthood was realized in the exercise of that power in the celebration of the eucharist and a mass celebrated by a bishop was no different from a mass celebrated by a priest. This view then held sway.

In the sixteenth century the Protestant reformers reacted to it by concentrating their attention on the universal priesthood of the baptized. The Council Fathers at Trent reacted to them. They concentrated instead on safeguarding priestly power by emphasizing even further the indelible character which was received at ordination. The essential difference between the clergy and the laity was marked more clearly. In these circumstances the cultic power acquired by the person ordained was all-important, while the significance of Scripture and the place of pastoral ministry itself were undervalued. This power was what mattered and it resided in the individual rather than the Church.

That in general was how ministerial priesthood was seen in the Catholic Church from the time of Trent until the Second Vatican Council. The emphasis was on cultic power, on the sacraments, rather than preaching the word, with the priest seen as another Christ, 'alter Christus'. Its strength lay in the importance it placed on personal holiness, but its view of ministry was narrow and its idea of community was weak.

I am keenly aware that this sketch is oversimplified.[1] From the earliest days the gospel has been proclaimed, the followers of Jesus have gathered to break bread in his memory, and, in spite of failings, at no time has the care of the faithful been utterly disregarded. The essential ministerial elements have always been exercised. I am not wishing to suggest anything else. In 1215, for example, the Fourth Lateran Council reaffirmed the fundamental place of preaching in the Church's ministry, declared for the first

1. For a more thorough and subtle account, see Paul Bernier, *Ministry in the Church: a Historical and Pastoral Approach* (Connecticut, 1992). I acknowledge gladly its influence on what I have offered here, but the sketch is my own responsibility.

time that the change in the bread and wine at the eucharist was a change of substance, and laid down instructions for the reform of the clergy to safeguard the quality of the ministry which the people should receive. But even then, although the bishops attended to the parts, they did not co-ordinate the vision. This sketch can help us realize that the understanding of ministry as word, service, and sacrament and the way these elements are related to one another has not always been clear. So, oversimplification notwithstanding, it is instructive to recognize, when we are specifically trying to grasp a deeper understanding of priestly ministry, that initially it was the preaching of the word which had pride of place; that that gave way in due course through the pressure of events – first, the growth and spread of the Church, then persecution, and then respectability – to priority being given to the element of service, expressed as leadership; and that that in its turn was overtaken by the emphasis placed on cultic power in order first to salvage the Church following the collapse of the Roman Empire, then to frustrate the ambitions of secular rulers, and finally to resist the protests of the Reformers. Over two thousand years different emphases have had their day, claiming predominance. It is amazing to realize that perhaps never until our own time has a deliberate attempt been made to put an integrated understanding of priestly ministry together.

We have come to recognize at last that word, service, and sacrament must go together; they are parts of a whole; they are not realities, independent in themselves, which we connect together to form something greater. And so, a preaching that ignored practice and celebration would be hollow and hypocritical; a ministry dislocated from its biblical roots and sacramental celebration would be a poor, emaciated thing, lacking substance and direction; and sacramental power which had become isolated, symbolizing neither word nor action, might be technically valid, but would in fact be enfeebled. The word that is preached should be celebrated in sacrament and made flesh in action. That is the vision of ministry offered by the Second Vatican Council and elaborated since then. We must first become aware of what we share, what makes us whole, before we can appreciate the separate parts.

And what is true for our understanding of these aspects of ministry is true as well for our understanding of ministry in relation to baptism.

(iv)

When the Protestant reformers sought to revive interest in the universal priesthood of the baptized, it was natural, as we have seen, for the Council Fathers at Trent to oppose them by emphasizing instead the essential distinction between clergy and laity so as to defend priestly powers. Controversy fuelled the conflict. But four hundred years later at the Second Vatican Council, away from the smoke of battle, it was possible to approach the matter more calmly. When the bishops there began to address the particular question of the ministry and life of priests, they felt able to start from what is held in common. They acknowledged, of course, that some people had been appointed as ministers; being set apart, however, did not make them separate (see *Presbyterorum Ordinis*, n. 3); and they declared first that in the Mystical Body, 'all the faithful are made a holy and kingly priesthood, they offer spiritual sacrifices to God through Jesus Christ, and they proclaim the virtues of him who has called them out of darkness into his admirable light' (*Presbyterorum Ordinis*, n. 2). There it is at once: a concern for all the people, coupled with reference to the three essential functions of priesthood, service, expressed as kingship, the offering of sacrifice, and proclamation. Before we can understand what is distinctive about ministerial priesthood, we must first recognize what all Christians have in common by virtue of their baptism.

It would be difficult to exaggerate the benefit of this approach. One of its advocates for many years was my friend, Michael Richards, who championed it regularly, particularly in his editorial contributions to *The Clergy Review*, but he perhaps expressed its value most succinctly in his book, *A People of Priests*, published shortly before he died. There he wrote:

> We need to start from what we are and what we have in common, and remain always aware of it throughout our analysis of the respective roles in the Church; otherwise, we shall overlook the very basis of our collaboration, and find ourselves using artificial and external means of organizing our joint action.

When we recognize what we share, it becomes easier to identify the different, particular parts which can contribute to the whole. To carry out this exercise the other way round leads to chaos. As Richards observed:

> If one starts from the separation of clergy and laity into two classes as a fact of life with which one has to work, and then seeks their closer collaboration, demarcation disputes inevitably arise, as they have done in the past, for example, over the apostolate of the laity, and as they are doing at the present moment over priesthood itself.[2]

We come to understand ministerial priesthood best when we begin by seeing it within the context of the common priesthood of all the baptized, not by trying to identify immediately what makes it different. I rejoice that I have been ordained, but I rejoice first of all that I have been baptized. And it is when that point is established that the relationship between the two priesthoods, the common and the ministerial, can be clarified.

(v)

In the Dogmatic Constitution on the Church, *Lumen Gentium*, the bishops at the Second Vatican Council declared that the common priesthood of the faithful and the ministerial priesthood

2. Michael Richards, *A People of Priests: the Ministry of the Catholic Church* (London, 1995), p. 60.

'differ essentially and not only in degree' (*Lumen Gentium*, n. 10). Since the time of that Council there has been much agonizing about this statement and about priestly identity. When so much emphasis is placed on the laity, ministerial priesthood can seem to lose its value and its purpose. What makes an ordained priest special? What constitutes the essential difference of which the document speaks? Here was another question close to Michael Richards' heart and I find his argument lucid and entirely persuasive. We used to talk about it, I have heard him preach on it, I have read his articles, and once again he gave it his particular attention in his final book. It requires attention to detail, but the effort is worthwhile.

The statement that these priesthoods 'differ essentially and not only in degree', could seem to suggest that the difference is in fact one of degree, and also of essence; that is to say, of essence as well as degree. In other words, the difference is of both degree and essence. If that is correct, it is easy to see how confusion could arise. Differences of degree imply that there is something greater and something less about the same thing; a difference of essence means that two realities are different altogether. There was a story Michael would tell with a mixture of amusement and frustration. He had been discussing this question with his bishop, Cardinal John Heenan, the Archbishop of Westminster. Heenan told him how he had explained it to the congregation at Westminster Cathedral by saying, 'We are all priests now in the Church. But you are little priests and I am a big priest.' Michael had been trying to make the point that the idea of degree – littleness and bigness – was what the Council had rejected, but he judged it more prudent to retire from the conversation at that point. Cardinal Heenan's misunderstanding is typical of the confusion which has tended to prevail. But the conciliar statement that the difference was essential, and 'not only in degree', or to follow the Latin original precisely, '*non gradu tantum*', that is, 'not in degree merely', implies at the very least an indifference to the question of degree, 'not a matter of mere degree'. In other words, degree has no importance. It may even imply that the question of degree is altogether irrelevant. The real difference is one of essence: when we are speaking about the common priesthood and the ministerial priesthood we are indeed speaking about two realities which are simply not the same. They are utterly and entirely different, because they are essentially different.

The problem, however, is complicated in English by our use of the same word, priest, to translate two different Greek words, πρεσβύτερος (in Latin, *presbyter*), meaning an elder or senior person, an office holder in the New Testament, and ἱερεύς (in Latin, *sacerdos*), referring to a priest in the Old Testament or the whole body of worshippers, the priestly people, in the New. We need to be sensitive to this distinction. Michael was rigorous in speaking of the ordained as presbyters and referring priesthood to the baptized. However, this usage is unfamiliar and can seem clumsy. In this book in general, I have used 'priest' in both contexts, but, where there might be misunderstanding, I have tried to ensure that my meaning is clear by speaking when necessary of ordained or ministerial priesthood, on the one hand, and the common or universal priesthood, on the other.[3]

It is vital to grasp that there is an essential difference between these two realities. Being different in essence means that these priesthoods are completely different. They are not the same. One is not a heightened version of the other; that would merely be a matter of degree. Baptism is not a basic participation in Christ which is brought to a greater fulfilment through presbyteral ordination; still less does presbyteral ordination override the common priesthood received in baptism. In a poetic progressive image, the French original of the *Catechism of the Catholic Church* speaks of baptism as 'le fondement de toute la vie chrétienne', the foundation stone of all Christian life, 'le porche de la vie dans l'Esprit', the porch of life in the Spirit, and 'la porte qui ouvre accès aux autres sacrements', the door which gives access to the other sacraments (*Catechism of the Catholic Church*, n.

3. See *ibid.*, pp. 5–7.

1213). The image of the porch is particularly telling. It is the place where we meet as equals.

It follows that those who are ordained do not slough off their membership of the common priesthood. St Augustine famously remarked, 'For you I am a bishop, with you I am a Christian' (*Sermon* 340, 1). Every ordained priest can adapt and echo his words, 'For you I am a presbyter, with you I am a Christian.' That is the great truth to be grasped and lived by. Baptism is fundamental. The distinctive service of ordained ministry is offered from within the common priesthood. But once that key distinction has been established, a further vital question remains. When the Second Vatican Council affirmed that these priesthoods are essentially distinct, it also described them as 'none the less ordered one to another' (*Lumen Gentium*, n. 10). So what is the relationship between them? How is that ordering to be understood? How should we define the distinctive identity of ministerial priesthood?

(vi)

I have a friend who is wise and perceptive. Sometimes, when we are discussing a difficult issue and, as it seems to me, he has made a particularly helpful remark, he will nevertheless pull me up short by observing, 'That's a description, not a judgement.' It's a valuable distinction. I am reminded of it here. It is what the Council Fathers seem to have been doing. They affirm the essential distinction between the two priesthoods and the fact that they are ordered one to another, but they then offer a description without providing an explanation. They just speak about the sacred power and rule exercised by the ordained and their celebration of the eucharist and about the faithful's participation. It is almost as though they know they are on to something, but aren't yet quite sure what it is. So they slip back into familiar turns of phrase.

Explanation and answer were offered very clearly, however, almost thirty years later in the *Catechism*. The question is put directly: in what sense are these two essentially different kinds of priesthood ordered to one another? And the answer is given: 'While the common priesthood of the faithful is exercised by the unfolding of baptismal grace . . . , the ministerial priesthood is at the service of the common priesthood' (*Catechism of the Catholic Church*, n. 1547). There you have it. Within the body of all the baptized, those who have been ordained are at the service of the rest, helping them to unfold the grace they have received, to nurture it, develop it, and deepen their life in Christ.

And how are they to do that? What kind of service are they to offer? First of all, they offer it by virtue of their ordination: they act in the person of Christ, their ministry depends entirely on his unique priesthood. And they do it as well because they act in the name of the whole Church: they are not its delegates, but, because they are ministers of Christ, of the whole Body of Christ, they are called ministers 'not only of Christ, but also of the Church' which is his Body (see *Catechism of the Catholic Church*, nn. 1548–53). These actions in the person of Christ and in the name of the Church form, therefore, the basis of their ministry. And so they preach the gospel to all, both formally in the liturgy and by taking other opportunities for teaching, and informally through missionary work or ordinary, daily conversation, as occasion may arise; they celebrate sacraments, baptizing, forgiving sins, anointing the sick, and celebrating mass; and they provide leadership to enable the community to reach its full and proper maturity in Christ (see *Presbyterorum Ordinis*, nn. 4–6). By carrying out these particular responsibilities, those who are presbyters, ministerial priests, give service to the universal priesthood of all the baptized. As Christ's representatives, they act for him as prophet when they preach, as priest when they celebrate sacraments, and as king when they lead and guide the community to new life in him. All that is straightforward enough. We have become familiar with it. And we rejoice that in our day as never before these elements of priestly ministry form an integrated vision.

But there is still a question which may nag away at us. Beautiful and elevated as this understanding of ministerial priesthood may be, we may wonder nevertheless about our identity. How are the ordained essentially different from those who are not? Some particular tasks are indeed reserved to us – presiding at the eucharist and speaking the words of consecration, absolving sins, and anointing those who are sick – but, wonderful and important as those sacramental actions are, are they in fact all that is different? It may seem so. We remember the words of Pope John Paul II in his Apostolic Exhortation on the vocation of the laity, *Christifideles Laici*: 'The participation of the lay faithful in the threefold mission of Christ as Priest, Prophet, and King finds its source in the anointing of Baptism, its further development in Confirmation, and its realization and dynamic sustenance in the Holy Eucharist.' Notice the progression: source, development, and sustenance. These are strong words. The laity too have their share in Christ as prophet, priest, and king. The Pope goes on to explain that this participation in Christ is given to each one individually, but that it derives from communion and is lived and realized in communion; in other words, it embraces both the individual and the community. And he concludes by quoting St Augustine: 'As we call everyone "Christians" in virtue of a mystical anointing, so we call everyone "priests" because all are members of one priesthood' (St Augustine, *De Civitate Dei*, 20, 10; see *Christifideles Laici*, n. 14). If you are an ordained priest and feeling depressed and perhaps a little cynical, you might well conclude from this that there is little which remains exclusive to the presbyter except the power to utter a few words, vital as they may be. Is that what we have come to? Is there nothing more to say? I believe there is.

(vii)

I suggest that we need to ask a different question if we are to discover the nature of the distinctive identity of those who have been ordained. We must ask what is the kind of identity we are trying to determine. Individuals are identified by what is exclusive to them, by what makes them unique, fingerprints and DNA. Is that the kind of identity we are trying to establish for the ordained? I think not. Their identity is not discovered by placing them in isolation, seeing them as individuals, but rather by seeing them in the context of the community. Think about communities, about groups or teams.

Muscular Christianity leaves many people cold. Denis Hickey, a priest of the Portsmouth Diocese, who was a student here at the Beda in the sixties, while I was at the English College, and whom I came to know much better later when we were both working in Oxford, used to describe with wry humour how his school chaplain would encourage them as boys to look upon Jesus as captain of the cricket team and try to rally their commitment by asking them to see themselves as members of his team who must bat and bowl and field for him. Denis was not impressed. The approach does not appeal. Yet there is something to be learnt from considering the way teams work.

To kick a football is to kick a football, whether you are the centre-forward, the goalkeeper, or the captain; a cover drive is a cover drive, whether you are the wicket-keeper, a fielder, a bowler, or, again, the captain; a serve and volley are the same whichever member of the Davis Cup team you may happen to be: individuals are identified by what makes them unique, but in a team much of what needs to be done is done by everyone. And it is the same in a community. If we try to establish someone's identity in community by examining principally what they do exclusively, we are not going to get very far. Identity within a community is not going to be discovered by concentrating primarily on an individual's exclusive activity. We need to approach the question in a different way.

What the captain of a sports team does may be much the same as everybody else, nevertheless there can be something particularly significant about him doing it. People sometimes remark, especially after a tight match, when a side has won against the odds, that the captain played 'a captain's game'. And they won't be meaning the way he spun the coin before the match began or even the way he varied the strategy and tactics as it developed, although that might come into it a little; they will be meaning rather that the way he played showed the others how they should play, inspired them, encouraged them, enabled them to lift their game so that they achieved the best possible result. I would want to say that it is something similar for those who have been ordained.

Of course, to say it again, ministerial priesthood involves particular responsibilities as well: we preach, we celebrate sacraments, and we offer leadership. I am not suggesting otherwise. But if we try to define our identity exclusively in those terms, we will soon run aground. All the baptized are prophets, priests, and kings; they must proclaim the gospel, make sacrifice, and offer leadership in society. To establish our identity within the community, however, we must realize that it is not determined by difference, but through ministry. At our ordination, we are not so much set apart to do things differently from everyone else, as called to do the same things, but explicitly in Christ's name.

Ministerial priesthood is a call to serve the common priesthood. We are not only to fulfil our particular responsibilities, but so to live our Christian lives that we are evident signs of Christ's abiding presence in our world. We are called, so to speak, 'to play a captain's game'.

All the baptized must proclaim the good news of Jesus Christ; and the preaching of the ordained, whether formally from a pulpit or informally by their lives, must not only inform and support them, but must be a witness which inspires them. The baptized make many sacrifices, because ordinary daily life is demanding. But they should find in the way the ordained celebrate sacraments, baptizing and absolving, presiding at the eucharist and anointing the sick, not to mention the way they handle their own hardships, evidence which helps them see more clearly that they are not alone: priests must be a sign to them and a reminder that Christ walks with them and shares their burdens. And the baptized offer leadership in their families and their wider relationships, at work and at play, championing a way of life built on justice and truth, on peace and love. Hard-bitten society may be sceptical, but Christian men and women are called to show that that is possible; and they should be able to look with confidence to their priests for guidance, because the lives of those who have been ordained must be established securely and unmistakably on those same principles. And there is something more.

People who want to find Jesus, should, of course, be able to find him in any Christian, but they should in particular be able to discover him in priests. We are meant to be the sacraments, the living signs, of his presence. They should be able to recognize him in our preaching and our praying, in the way we celebrate sacraments, and in the way we care for them and give them service; but most of all they should see him in the way we live our lives day by day, in our own deliberate, conscious commitment to Christ. By ordination, as the Second Vatican Council declared, there is a sense in which priests are segregated from the People of God, set apart, but they are not, therefore, separated from them; they are to remain in their midst (see *Presbyterorum Ordinis*, n. 3). Little that we actually do will be different from the actions of everyone else. We don't discover our identity in our different actions, but by our being commissioned as living signs of Christ's presence. Let us take stock.

(viii)

A vocation to ministerial priesthood is no guarantee of perfection. I state the obvious: the ordained are not preserved from sin. At the same time, all the baptized are called to bear witness to Christ's presence. Holy people, whoever they may be, offer us glimpses of that presence. They don't have to have been ordained.

I think, for example, of Donald Nicholl whom I knew for twenty-five years, but met too rarely. He died in 1997. He was a husband, a father, and a grandfather. He came from Yorkshire and he loved cricket, so there are no surprises there. He was a humble man and a gifted, imaginative scholar, and he was passionate about justice and truth. If you have never heard of him and want to capture a sense of what he was like, then read his account of his time as Rector of the Ecumenical Institute for Theological Research at Tantur between Jerusalem and Bethlehem. He was Rector from 1981 to 1985. He called this journal *The Testing of Hearts*.[4] As a record of one man's dealings with Jew, Christian, and Muslim in most delicate circumstances, it is unequalled. His care and respect for everyone are constant; he confronts difficulties bravely, but he will not be bamboozled; and he chronicles with humble precision his own mistakes, limitations, and failures. His example inspires and instructs me.

I last spoke to him by telephone not long before he died. He was tired and weak, but he roused himself to talk a little and told me that he was trying to prepare himself to die well. It was a modest description, not a boast. And he reminded me about the ending of Bernanos's *Diary of a Country Priest*: 'Tout est grâce, everything is grace.' I think Donald was a saint, because, it seems to me, his presence cast light on what Jesus must have been like. In his company it was impossible not to share his passion for justice and truth. His integrity gave birth to integrity in others. I think the presence of Jesus must have been like that. There must have been something compelling about it. As it was impossible to lie to Donald, or behave hypocritically, or pretend to a knowledge you did not have, because the hollowness and artificiality, the unreality, would have been exposed at once, so, I believe, it would have been impossible in the presence of Jesus. Donald's presence had that Christlike quality. It is not something reserved for the ordained.

What I saw in Donald, however, is a way of living which by virtue of my ordination I am committed to follow. What I was blessed to find in him, others should expect to find in me. The

4. See Donald Nicholl, *The Testing of Hearts: a Pilgrim's Journal*, new edition (London, 1998).

prospect is daunting. How can anyone be expected to match that expectation? But that is the call of ministerial priesthood. The witness of the ordained is the fruit of deliberate commitment. How we live should disclose who we are. We are meant to be living signs of Christ's presence. It is an overwhelming vocation. How can we be capable of it?

5

A Human Calling

(i)

In August 1967 I went on holiday with a group of friends to Salzburg. One of them was David Standley. David had been ordained a few weeks earlier and said mass for us each day. While we were there, we celebrated the feast of St Augustine and I have never forgotten the brief homily he preached that day. He reminded us of the part played by St Ambrose in Augustine's conversion. It was vital. And what had Ambrose done? What had he said? When these men met who were destined with Jerome and Gregory the Great to be regarded as the great Fathers of the Latin Church, what telling argument had Ambrose used which persuaded and convinced Augustine of the truth of the Christian faith? The answer is, he had used none. What touched Augustine, first of all, was his kindness. He 'received me like a father', Augustine wrote, 'and expressed pleasure at my coming with a kindness most fitting in a bishop.' The arguments at this stage made no impression. 'I began to like him,' he continued, 'at first indeed not as a teacher of the truth, for I had absolutely no confidence in your Church, but as a human being who was kind to me.'[1] Human kindness was the key. That was David's point. What was achieved later began by being built on a basic human quality. That truth is inescapable.

Those ordained to ministerial priesthood may be expected to be living signs of Christ's presence, as we have noticed, and that may seem very exalted; nevertheless, in the first place this

1. Augustine, *Confessions* V.xiii (23), tr. Henry Chadwick (Oxford, 1991), p. 88.

vocation is a human calling. That point is fundamental. We have to be well-rounded human beings. It stands to reason. If we are to be signs of Christ's presence, of the Word made flesh, of the divine in the human, what is the condition of that humanity in which the divine is to make its home? If grace is to build on nature and so bear fruit, that nature needs to be in good repair. To quote Peter Steele, the Australian Jesuit poet and writer, 'no good surgeon is going to try to transplant onto gangrenous tissue'.[2]

Awareness of this question has come to prominence in recent years. At the Synod on priestly formation which was held in Rome in 1990, a proposition was put together which was adopted in the Papal document which followed it: 'The whole work of priestly formation would be deprived of its necessary foundation if it lacked a suitable human formation' (*Propositio* 21, quoted in *Pastores Dabo Vobis*, n. 43). The other areas of formation identified in the document are spiritual, intellectual, and pastoral; they have a crucial part to play and no one should underestimate their importance. Nothing said here is meant to compromise their significance. This statement is declaring that what we build in those areas is built on sand, unless the human base is secure. Sound human formation is indispensable. Anyone who has thought seriously about preparing people for ministry will recognize that.

Those who come to discern their vocation and prepare for ordination are good people. Of course, there can be exceptions, but they are rare. These are fine individuals. In general, they will be devoted to developing the spiritual life; they may not all be brilliant scholars, but they will be interested in study for the sake of their ministry, and they will be committed to the service of those in need. To put it simply, when it comes to prayer, flair, and care, they will normally pass the test with ease. When problems arise, it will almost invariably be something related to

2. Peter Steele SJ, *Bread for the Journey: Homilies* (Melbourne, 2002), p. 36.

human formation. And the issue is serious, because human nature isn't changed by ordination. Grace builds on nature. It doesn't replace it. We remain the people we are.

The continuity is most immediately obvious when we think about our limitations. Timothy Dolan, who is now the Archbishop of Milwaukee, was Rector of the North American College in Rome for seven years. His comments capture this point trenchantly. He pulls no punches. If a seminarian is lazy, Dolan remarks, 'he will be a lazy priest'. And so he goes on:

> A crab as a seminarian? Another crabby priest!
> A slob as a seminarian? A slob as a priest!
> Always late before ordination? You'll irritate people by not being on time as a priest.
> A shy seminarian who avoids people? Someone unlikely to do the aggressive evangelization the Church expects of her priests.
> Someone with b.o. and bad breath? A priest people will avoid.
> Someone who bores people silly with incessant chatter? People won't answer their doors when you come visit.
> A gossip as a seminarian? So we will have another flannel-mouth priest!
> Someone who flies off the handle at the slightest thing? Another mean priest![3]

What is stated here about the idle and the ill-tempered, the uncouth, the unpunctual, and the unwashed, the painfully shy and the tiresomely boring, the gossip and the self-centred, doesn't pretend to exhaust the possibilities, but, when expressed as starkly as that, the fundamental importance of human formation is plain. Too many people have had to deal with the priests such students have become for further evidence to need to be called.

3. Timothy M. Dolan, *Priests for the Third Millennium* (Huntington, 2000), p. 146.

However, the question is not entirely straightforward. That there should be such weaknesses and limitations doesn't necessarily matter in itself, provided a person will acknowledge them and work to overcome them. The difficulty occurs when they are disguised and denied; then they are like a time-bomb, waiting to explode. When in particular they are the result of sexual dysfunction, the damage they can cause, as we know all too well, is devastating and its effects uncontrollable. From this perspective to be a priest is, first of all, a human calling, a call to become a whole and mature human being.

(ii)

Maturity is a matter of self-knowledge. To be mature we don't need to know ourselves perfectly; we spend our entire lives growing in self-knowledge; but we have to acquire sufficient self-knowledge at least. Healthy people have a proper level of self-awareness. They take pride in their strengths and are realistic about their limitations. A limitation is not necessarily a weakness; it may be, but it doesn't have to be. We all have limitations; no one is perfect. We need to get the balance right.

Sometimes people who lack maturity are described as filled with self-hatred. That seems rather violent. What does it mean? We sometimes see people who may be askew, although they don't seem obviously to be raging against themselves. Self-hatred in this context, however, is not about raging. It refers rather to that lack of balance. Those who hate themselves are refusing to accept themselves as they are, to come to terms with their own reality, proud of their gifts, honest about their flaws. Maturity means coming to terms with ourselves. We can easily be handicapped by pretending to a state which in fact we have not attained, and, if we aren't honest with ourselves about it, we will never be free to deal with it. We have to accept who we are, both the good and the bad.

It is instructive to notice the negative; when it occurs, it reveals the significance of our human qualities very clearly. A self-serving seminarian will be a self-serving priest. We need, however, to be aware of the positive as well. We can rewrite Dolan's list from another perspective:

> A generous seminarian? A generous priest.
> A courteous seminarian? A courteous priest.
> Someone who is punctual before ordination? Someone people will feel respects them.
> Someone whose care for others makes him master his shyness and reserve? Someone whose pastoral ministry will be valued. (Bishop Eric Grasar, who was the Bishop of Shrewsbury and ordained me, was a naturally shy man. You could see it at a glance. However, I remember him remarking, 'Shyness is not a pastoral virtue.' He had worked to conquer his natural reserve.)
> Someone who dresses and behaves appropriately, according to the situation? Someone people feel they can approach.
> Someone who knows when to listen as well as when to speak? Someone people will welcome to their homes.
> Someone who can keep a confidence? Someone people feel they can trust.
> Someone who is patient under stress? An example to admire.

Pastores Dabo Vobis addresses the same point and names qualities which are valuable in themselves and valuable for pastoral ministry too: a love for the truth, loyalty, respect for others, a sense of justice, honesty and reliability, compassion, integrity, and balanced judgement and behaviour (see n. 43). Once again, as with bad habits, so with good ones: those who love truth, are loyal, respect others, work for justice, and so forth before ordination are likely to be the same afterwards. The list may seem formidable. It is. We are being summoned to a care for others which is combined with a steadfast commitment to justice and truth. It may also seem rather abstract. We need to put flesh on its skeleton.

(iii)

When St Paul descants on love in his first letter to the Corinthians, he declares that the gift of many languages, the understanding of profound mystery, the faith to move mountains, and even a readiness to sacrifice your life are worthless without love. And then he identifies love with everyday human qualities, like kindness and patience and rejoicing in the right (see 1 Corinthians 13:1–6). Now consider Jesus' meetings with three women.

We are told that one day, in the midst of a great crowd, a woman who for years has had a flow of blood, probably excessive haemorrhaging when she menstruates during her monthly period, makes her way through the throng to touch the edge of his clothes, believing that, if she can do so, she will be cured. And she does. And she is. But Jesus is aware that something special has happened, 'that power had gone forth from him', and asks who has touched him. The disciples think the question absurd because of the press of people, but he insists and the woman finally comes forward 'in fear and trembling'. She may be in awe of the healing she has received or fearful that, given her condition, in touching him she has involved him in ritual uncleanness (see Leviticus 15:19–30). Does she fear his anger? But Jesus listens to her story, praises her faith, and sends her away with a blessing of peace (see Mark 5:24–34). As well as healing her, he shows her great kindness.

People sometimes make their way to priests. They are not obviously in fear and trembling, but they are perhaps more nervous than they seem. Someone they love has died, a parent, a husband or wife, a partner, a child, or a dear friend. They are Catholics, but not particularly practising. Nor was the deceased. They would like a church funeral, if possible, a requiem mass, but they are not sure at all of the procedures. How are they received? There are priests who say, 'Why should I bother with them? They never came here before. Why should I put myself out?' They refuse to celebrate a mass and arrange the briefest ceremony possible at the cemetery or crematorium; they do not preach, and they scarcely offer any word of comfort. But there are others who seize the opportunity. They listen without judging and plan with care a funeral which pays proper tribute to the one who has died. To preach may not be easy; it may best be likened to making bricks without straw; and yet, as they listen to the dead person's family and friends, they hear a story or two which suggests something of the character of the person who has died. It is possible to make something of that. And they do. Those who are mourning find that they have been comforted and are truly grateful. Sometimes they will say, 'He really caught him', when in his homily the priest has done little more than reshape and feed back to them what they had reported to him. Whatever theological issues may be involved, simple kindness has had an effect. Sometimes afterwards people return to the practice of the faith. More often they do not. But they appreciate the care they have received, and who knows what seeds have been sown and how they will flower in the future. As Ambrose with Augustine, kindness makes a world of difference.

Then there is the woman at the well in Samaria. In this case Jesus takes the initiative. He speaks to her. He asks her for a drink. The conversation takes off from there. It is often taken as a model for catechesis, showing how people should be approached on their terms, rather than on terms which we have selected for them. The point is well made, yet her questions and comments can also be seen as over-confident and rather tiresome: why are you, a Jew, speaking to me, a Samaritan? Where is your cup to draw the living water? I don't have a husband. Where should we worship, on the mountain or in Jerusalem? (See John 4:7–42.) But Jesus keeps his patience and is consistently kind to her. Finally, she calls her friends and neighbours who come to appreciate him for themselves. Patience and kindness will often go hand in hand. We need to be patient as well.

Some years ago a couple visited a priest I know. They came reluctantly and grudgingly. They were planning to be married in the beautiful local Anglican parish church, but the vicar who had spent some time helping them prepare, when he discovered that the man was a Catholic, sent them round to see this priest so that they could also prepare themselves with him and obtain the necessary dispensation for their Anglican wedding. But they were not happy. The meeting did not begin easily because the couple felt it was an imposition. They were even less happy when they discovered there would have to be several meetings. However, the priest took a deep breath, contained his impatience, explained the significance of their meeting him as well, and tried to engage them in conversation. As it happened, he was more successful than he would have dared hope at the beginning. During the second meeting the couple asked him if he would attend their wedding, to read a prayer or perhaps even to preach. When they came the third time, they were regretting that he could not officiate. They returned to speak to the vicar who most generously agreed that they could alter their arrangements. And so in the end the priest officiated instead of the vicar. The story is not told to score points – whether the marriage rite was to be Anglican or Catholic is immaterial – but as an example of the way patience and kindness can win people over.

Thirdly, there was the woman taken in adultery. Jesus is teaching in the Temple when some scribes and Pharisees bring a woman who has been caught committing adultery, and they ask him a question. They are not particularly interested in her. They want to test him. According to the law of Moses, she should be stoned; the Romans forbade them using the death penalty; whose side is Jesus on? It is a trap. If he supports the Mosaic law, he is at odds with the Romans; if he doesn't, he can be disowned. But Jesus bends down and writes in the dust, though what that gesture means is unclear, and then he stands up and says to them, 'Let him who is without sin among you be the first to throw a stone at her.' He stoops down once more and continues writing, and they slip away, one by one. Finally, alone with the woman, Jesus asks, 'Has no one condemned you?' She says to him, 'No one, Lord.' And he says, 'Neither do I condemn you.' He is not among her accusers. He sends her away and instructs her to sin no more (see John 8:2–11). Here Jesus is not only being kind, as well as skilful in avoiding the trap set for him, nor is he merely forgiving sin: on this occasion, I would suggest, he is also rejoicing in the right. He wants the woman to be able to move on. It is a model for a priest hearing confessions.

People sometimes wonder what that must be like. One of the common questions a priest is asked is whether he remembers what he has been told in confession. Speaking for myself, but I don't imagine I'm exceptional, I would answer generally, 'No, I do not', and for two reasons. The first is the more obvious: over the years I have heard far too many confessions to be able to, and by and large the sins people commit are not original. But, secondly and far more importantly, I am not listening in order to remember: I am listening in order to help. Sometimes I wish I could remember better. A person comes in and speaks with shame and sorrow about the wrong she has done. It is a painful story, perhaps about the resentment she feels for someone she should love. And here is the point, it has taken her a long time to find the courage to tell her story and confess. We speak. I give her absolution. She is grateful and leaves. But the situation itself is not resolved at once. And so, some weeks later, I hear again the same voice: 'Hello, Father. You remember what I was telling you last time.' And I don't. I recognize the voice, but I don't remember because I wasn't listening to remember. And so unfortunately she is forced to revisit her pain once more. I would rather spare her that. She may not need to tell me the whole tale, but she will have to jog my memory. In the confessional, a priest is not listening to remember, but to discover what is positive. We give absolution and try to help those who repent to be healed, so that like the woman taken in adultery they can move on. Our purpose is not to cast judgement, but to rejoice in the right.

In these three meetings, wonderful things can be said to be happening, healing, insight into a person's life, forgiveness; but human qualities are also being exercised, kindness, patience, and generosity. These are the human marks of the love Paul praises. But that too cannot be the whole story. If it were, it would all be too nice. There are difficult moments in life as well. It is not always possible simply to be kind, patient, and positive. We may have to confront injustice.

There was an occasion when Jesus went into the Temple and, when he saw the money-changers and the people who had turned its precincts into a market, he made a whip of cords and drove them out. He was filled with anger. 'You shall not make my Father's house,' he told them, 'a house of trade' (see John 2:14–22). In the Synoptic Gospels it is the incident which triggers his arrest, torture, and execution, but in the Fourth Gospel it occurs right at the beginning of his public ministry. Scholars wonder which version is the more accurate historically. If the Johannine account is more correct, I wonder whether this was Jesus' first visit to the Temple since that occasion, according to St Luke, when he was twelve and had been found there by Mary and Joseph after three days. Had customs deteriorated in the intervening years? Or perhaps the twelve-year-old had not noticed what was going on. Now he was appalled. Was his anger an outburst of spontaneous emotion because of what he found? He could not contain himself. It is impossible to know, but there is still a lesson to be learnt.

We can't always be nice. There is a place for anger. There is no place for it when it is simply self-regarding, my way of reacting when I am not getting what I want. That anger is the deadly sin. But to see injustice or wrong-doing and not challenge it, because it doesn't affect me or would not serve my interest, would itself be wrong. Then lack of anger would be sinful, unhealthy repressed emotion. We must not fear our emotions. Another mark of maturity is the ability to deal constructively with them. To protest may take courage; it is natural to feel fearful when we have to confront; but the failure to act would reveal weakness and immaturity. There can be a need for steel. We have to be kind and patient and positive, but we must also have a sense of justice and be people of integrity who are prepared to stand up in the cause of right, whatever the cost.

These human qualities, well integrated, indicate maturity. They make us steady, reliable, trustworthy people. They also mirror Jesus, who was not, St Paul tells us, 'Yes and No; but in him it is always Yes' (2 Corinthians 1:19). Paul's declaration is powerful. It points to that very steadiness, trustworthiness, reliability in Jesus. It touches particularly our human calling. It supplies a context. What are we to make of it? It is helpful to consider this Yes of Jesus. There are three immediate lessons we can learn.

(iv)

The Yes of Jesus speaks, first of all, of his constancy. Some people dither and are indecisive; they can never make their minds up. Others, once a decision has been made, refuse to change it, however mistaken they can be shown to be; they are stubborn, perhaps because they are stupid, or perhaps because they dread, as they see it, losing face. 'Jesus Christ was not Yes and No.' He didn't dither. 'In him it is always Yes'. But that Yes is not stubbornness. We are at a deeper level. His constancy is a mark of maturity. A wise decision, maintained faithfully, is a sign of a well-integrated personality. A course has been set and its consequences will be accepted. It is a matter of living at depth. A familiar image returns: those who are constant can move with the undertow, they are not bobbing about on the surface. They are not manipulating events to get what they like on their own terms, shifting and twisting. The Yes of Jesus speaks of constancy.

It is also positive, affirmative. It seeks the good in people, like Jesus with the woman taken in adultery. Jack Pledger once told me that St Francis de Sales used to say there is good in everyone, and the fun lies in discovering it. I've never found the exact quotation, but the idea rings true. It is not naïve advice. It makes me think of Barry Nicholas.

Barry Nicholas died in March, 2002. He was a distinguished

man in many ways, as an academic, a teacher, and as Principal of Brasenose College, Oxford, from 1978 to 1989. The Oxford University Catholic Chaplaincy was his parish and he was generous with his time on its behalf. I first got to know him in 1970, when I went to live there, newly ordained, as a graduate. Later my time as chaplain coincided almost exactly with his as Principal. He was then no longer able to continue as chairman of the Chaplaincy Trustees, but he remained a source of wise advice, good humour, and friendship. We had last exchanged cards and messages the Christmas before he died. But what was remarkable about Barry Nicholas, what made him so distinguished, was not simply the things he did, but the kind of person he was. At his Memorial Service in Oxford a year later, Lord Mark Saville, a former pupil, paid him this tribute:

> [His] character engendered affection and respect in equal and very great measure from all who were privileged to meet and get to know him. The affection arose from the fact that Barry Nicholas was a person who took a genuine interest in those that he met, going out of his way to help and advise, with no selfish motive but only a kind desire to give what he could, which was much. The respect arose from the fact that he constantly demonstrated that gentleness is not the same as weakness, that quietness and calmness are preferable to loudness and aggression, and that when wisdom is allied with those qualities (as it was with him) more can be achieved than by any other means.

Here was a man who followed the advice of Francis de Sales. He was positive. He looked for the good in people and sought to extract it with kindness, gentleness, and patience. And in all that there was no trace of weakness.

When that constancy and readiness to be positive are combined, the Yes of Jesus is also healing. Think again of the woman taken in adultery, who is finally sent away with her sins forgiven and instructed to sin no more; think of the paralytic who is lowered through the roof by his friends, whose sins also are forgiven and who is told to take up his stretcher and go home (see Mark 2:1–12); think of Bartimaeus, the blind beggar, who refuses to be discouraged by the crowd's disapproval, is greeted by Jesus, and sent on his way with his sight restored (see Mark 10:46–52). These miracle stories are not merely examples of divine power working through Jesus; they also illustrate the way his ordinary humanity had a part to play.

(v)

When the call to priestly ministry is recognized as a calling which is human as well as divine, we find that it is telling us something about our relationship with ourselves, our relationship with God, and our relationship with others. The Yes of Jesus as constant, positive, and healing can be understood as corresponding to those three relationships.

The Yes which is constant refers to ourselves: constancy reveals maturity, appropriate self-knowledge, a well-integrated person. That should be clear. The Yes which is positive, which affirms, which seeks the good in others, brings us close to God. How? In this context I have referred to Barry Nicholas. Let me return to him again. His obituary in *The Times* called him 'a power for good in individual lives'. It described the way he chaired the disciplinary committee, following the serious student unrest in the early seventies: 'In his patience and tolerance there was no trace of dissimulation. Day after day he absorbed abuse and unreason, and was neither disturbed nor disillusioned'; and it declared that 'he belonged in the tradition which regards those in power as servants of those they command. And every section of the community benefited from that commitment'.[4] These remarks capture the man well. I would say further that they point to his faith, the depth of his closeness to God. And the third aspect of this Yes, the one which heals, is significant for our relationship with others. It is the fruit of what has gone

4. *The Times*, 7 March 2002.

before. Those who are self-possessed, but self-effacing, and seek what is good, find that they reconcile where previously there was conflict. Again, Barry Nicholas comes to mind. To quote the obituary once more, 'his indifference to personal glory made him master of the art of giving others the impression that it was they who had hit upon his solution or had inspired the felicitous form of words to which all could assent'. He resolved problems without really being noticed. It is a matter of integration. Here too what is found among the laity can inspire the priest. What we find in them, others must be able to find in us.

To be called to ministerial priesthood is a human, as well as a divine, calling. With us too it must always be Yes. Our own maturity and our intimacy with God shape the way we can relate to others. Pope John Paul II has affirmed, 'Of special importance is the capacity to relate to others' (*Pastores Dabo Vobis*, n. 43). It is a subject which deserves particular attention. How are we to relate to others and do so with love? It raises a further factor. In our tradition those who are ordained are usually called also to be celibate. And so the question is still more precise: how are we to be both loving and celibate?

6

Loving and Celibate

(i)

ONE December morning, some years ago, I went to have my hair cut. The barber and I chatted. I was working at the Oxford Chaplaincy at the time. She wondered what I would be doing over Christmas because, of course, the University was on vacation. I explained that it would make little difference. A third of the students were graduates, many from overseas who would not be returning home. Then there were the dons who taught in the University and their families, the administrators, librarians, domestic staff, and others for whom the Chaplaincy was their parish. There would be midnight mass, two masses in the morning, and then in the evening a gathering for a traditional Christmas dinner with all the trappings, particularly for overseas students and families of friends. There were never fewer than thirty people at the table, sometimes more than fifty. The barber took all this in. She was impressed. Then she asked, 'Is there anything you can't do?' 'Well,' I replied, 'I can't get married.' She nearly dropped the scissors.

Fewer people in countries like Britain and the United States may be choosing to marry these days, but many find the idea that the option is not even available impossible to understand. I have been celibate all my life. Before I began my training for the priesthood in 1963, I remember a priest I admired asking me what I thought the hardest part of a priest's life would be. I answered, 'Not being married.' He agreed. But, although I was able to give that answer and accept celibacy not merely as a necessary undertaking in order to be ordained, but positively, deliberately, and willingly, I know now that I had little appreciation of the commitment I was making.

Does that invalidate my young decision? I don't think so. As the years pass, my appreciation of celibacy grows. It does not become any easier, at times it is harder, but I understand it better and value it more. It is also important to keep matters in perspective. The answer to the question, 'Wouldn't you like to be married?', is after all, 'Not to most people.' At the same time, I don't suppose I'm the only priest who smiles to himself while saying his breviary in the seventh week of what we call Ordinary Time. The Scripture for that week in the Office of Readings is taken from the book of Ecclesiastes. On the Friday I find I am commanded, 'Spend your life with the woman you love' (Ecclesiastes 9:9 Jerusalem Bible).

In the early nineties, celibacy itself became rather fashionable. The newspapers seemed to feature articles regularly about celebrities who were frightened of AIDS or recovering from unhappy love affairs, or workaholics who had no desire to waste their energy on sex. But they were taking time out. They were celibate in fact for the moment. They weren't committed to celibacy. Commitment seems bizarre. Yet commitment is the issue. That is something altogether different.

In the discussions surrounding celibacy in the Church today, one particular line of argument supports the view that celibacy should be the result of a free choice, not just in the sense that those who are ordained act freely, but something more than that: they should be free to choose whether as priests they will be celibate or not. The witness of celibacy, it is urged, will be more clearly visible when it is not undertaken as part of a package. It is a significant point. On the other hand, to abandon the law which requires celibacy of those to be ordained, could also be said to weaken its witness. If celibacy were to become simply a matter of personal choice, it could then be indistinguishable from a preference for remaining unmarried. As Raymond Brown once observed, 'Some of the forms of optional celibacy being proposed would soon lead to obscuring the vocational character of celibacy and would reduce it to a personal idiosyncrasy.'[1]

Those who make a commitment to be celibate and try to live according to it, however inadequately, are taking seriously the risk of discipleship. In an Anglican sermon, John Henry Newman once asked, 'What have we ventured for Christ?'[2] He was asking people to consider how would they be any the worse off, if Christ's promise were proved to be false. It is a question all Christians should ask themselves. Those who are committed to celibacy, know at least part of the answer. The lack of intimacy, the lack of family, children of my own, the solitude which can fray into loneliness, the fear of an isolated old age, these are things which those who never marry have to put up with in any case, but which celibates embrace deliberately. We are ready to make the sacrifice. What foolishness if the promise is false. We take the risk for Christ's sake.

(ii)

The origins of commitment to celibacy are to be found in the person of Jesus of Nazareth. He had come to make the Father's love known, to proclaim that the kingdom of heaven was close at hand. That mission absorbed him. He never married. Direct scriptural evidence is slight, but reference is commonly made to a scene in St Matthew's Gospel.

The Pharisees question him about the possibility of divorce. He reminds them of the teaching in the book of Genesis, based on an understanding of creation, about a man leaving his father and mother and being joined to his wife and the two becoming one. 'What therefore God has joined together,' he concludes, 'let not man put asunder.' They press him, quizzing him about Moses' acceptance of divorce. He explains that that teaching was

1. Raymond Brown, *Priest and Bishop: Biblical Reflections* (New York, 1970), p. 26.
2. J.H. Newman, *Parochial and Plain Sermons* iv, uniform edition (Westminster, 1967), p. 301.

because of their hardness of heart and that it was not so from the beginning. The disciples are bowled over. The teaching that seems to eliminate a second chance at marrying, if the first goes wrong, is so demanding they wonder who would ever marry. The risk seems too high. He tells them that such a commitment to marriage – he is explaining his own teaching, what we will call Christian marriage – is a gift not given to everyone. Then there is the famous eunuch saying: 'For there are eunuchs who have been so from birth, and there are eunuchs who have been made eunuchs by men, and there are eunuchs who have made themselves eunuchs for the sake of the kingdom of heaven' (Matthew 19:3–12). In other words, there are some people who do not wish to marry, some who may not be able to, and some, deserted by those whom they had married, who choose not to marry again because of their commitment to the kingdom. The passage, as it stands, is about marriage, not celibacy.

So why bother with it? Because, as Francis Moloney has argued most persuasively when explaining this text and discussing this issue, the abusive term 'eunuch' remains significant here, but for different reasons. This crude expression was most probably retained because it was actually used. The smear was levelled at Jesus, this man who disturbed the establishment and failed to follow the instruction to increase and multiply (see Genesis 1:28). He remained unmarried. And he accepted the abuse, but turned it round. He was a eunuch, not because of any physical incapacity, but for the sake of the kingdom. His mission so overwhelmed him that he had energy and attention for nothing else, not even marriage.[3] And there were soon disciples who followed him.

Paul was such a person. Writing to the Corinthians, no more than thirty years after the death of Jesus and his resurrection, he declares, 'I wish that all were as I myself am.' He is referring to

3. See Francis J. Moloney, *Disciples and Prophets: a Biblical Model for the Religious Life* (London, 1980), pp. 105–14. I find Moloney's reflections on Matthew 19 entirely convincing and gladly acknowledge my debt to him.

his not being married, his freedom from all anxiety, except 'the affairs of the Lord' (see 1 Corinthians 7:7, 32–5). That is how he wishes everyone else to be. More immediately, of course, he is writing in the context of expecting the second coming of Jesus at any moment. He believes that the kingdom is about to be realized soon. It is better, he is saying, to concentrate on that. All the same, he recognizes that there are people for whom that may not be possible. His own commitment, however, was not governed by practicalities, his – in fact, mistaken – conviction about Jesus' imminent return. He was overwhelmed by his desire to serve Christ, he wanted absolutely to be free for that, to devote himself to the Lord's affairs without reserve. That was the essential nature of his commitment.

None the less, we know that it was not a law for all. Those with responsibility for the early communities did not have to be celibate. Those called bishops were to be husbands 'of one wife' (1 Timothy 3:2). Some scholars today would argue that these men were in fact widowers; when their wives had died, they had not remarried, because to have done so would have indicated a lack of undivided commitment, which made them unsuitable for office. There is no need to resolve that dispute here. Whether true or false, it is certainly the case that celibacy for the sake of the kingdom was valued even from the earliest times.

Then, as attitudes towards sexuality changed and became more negative and as monastic asceticism developed, celibacy came to be insisted upon more and more. This ground is familiar. The dates too are well known: in 305 the Council of Elvira decreed that priests could be married, but had to abstain from sexual relations with their wives; the Council of Nicea in 325, preoccupied as it was with the Arian controversy, found time nevertheless to proclaim that no one, once ordained a deacon, was allowed to marry; in 925 at the Council of Spalatro, although a priest could be married, were his wife to die, he was not permitted to marry again; in 1123 at the First Lateran Council the law of celibacy as such was required of the clergy for the first time, but much ignored in the centuries that followed; then, at the Council of

Trent, the twenty-fourth session on 11 November 1563 reaffirmed vigorously the law on clerical celibacy by condemning as invalid the marriages of clerics who had vowed themselves to chastity; and the Second Vatican Council once again confirmed that teaching in 1965, emphasizing the harmony between celibacy and ministerial priesthood (see *Presbyterorum Ordinis*, n. 16). It is instructive to recognize the shape of the argument for celibacy throughout history.

No one suggests celibacy is essential to priesthood. It is a law of the Church. The Eastern Church has a long tradition of ordaining married men as deacons and priests, while more recent popes, Pius XII, Paul VI, and John Paul II, have dispensed from celibacy married priests and ministers of other Christian traditions in the West who, after their reception into full communion, have been ordained to continue their ministry as Catholic priests. Nevertheless, its origins are discovered in the example of Jesus himself and those who are ordained are called to be signs of his presence. The ministerial priesthood is a real sharing in the unique priesthood of Christ (see *Lumen Gentium*, n. 2). Ordination establishes a relationship between the ordained and Christ which cannot be undone. The tradition speaks of it conferring a mark or, more technically, a sacramental character. Once someone has been ordained, although they may later be dispensed from continuing their ministry or indeed forbidden to exercise it, that relationship cannot be annulled. A particular bond with Christ has been established. That bond supplies the basis from which the harmony between this way of life and celibacy can be most readily perceived. The celibate state bears witness to a dedication to serve people with an undivided heart; it makes possible a greater freedom to serve; that service seeks to bring about the mystical marriage between Christ and all the faithful who are his Bride, the Church; and the priest's own commitment to celibacy is itself a sign of the world to come, anticipated in human society in every generation (see *Presbyterorum Ordinis*, n. 16).

Specific reasons in support of celibacy have varied throughout the history of the Church, notably a long period during which human sexuality was regarded as soiled, as inextricably handicapped by sinfulness, and so was seen as inappropriate for those who ministered at the altar. But there is a pattern which emerges: the ideal revealed by Jesus; the bond between Jesus and the ordained, which came to be expressed in terms of sacramental character and illustrated by celibacy; the freedom and pastoral availability which celibacy created, enabling the priest to fulfil his ministry more perfectly. The priest was a sign here and now of faith in the world to come where there would be neither marrying nor giving in marriage. And it is this vision of the value and virtue of celibacy which has been sealed by church law.

This account of the origins and history of celibacy is altogether familiar. There is more that could be said and there are points which can be disputed, particularly the claim that the unmarried are necessarily more available for pastoral service, but those are the essential elements. More recently, however, a further element has been added which makes a significant difference.

(iii)

In *Pastores Dabo Vobis*, after speaking of priesthood as a human calling, Pope John Paul II turned to the question of what he called 'affective maturity'. He described it as 'the result of an education in true and responsible love'. He went on to say that affective maturity 'presupposes an awareness that love has a central role in human life', and he then quoted his own first Encyclical Letter, *Redemptor hominis*. There he stated:

> Man cannot live without love. He remains a being that is incomprehensible for himself, his life is meaningless, if love is not revealed to him, if he does not encounter love, if he does not experience it and make it his own, if he does not participate intimately in it.

These are powerful words and the Pope evidently wanted to be sure he was not going to be misunderstood. And so he explained,

> We are speaking of a love that involves the entire person, in all his aspects, physical, psychic, and spiritual, and which is expressed in the 'nuptial meaning' of the human body, thanks to which a person gives himself to another and takes the other to himself. A properly understood sexual education leads to understanding and realizing this 'truth' about human love. (*Pastores Dabo Vobis*, nn. 43–4)

This kind of recognition of the place of love in the life of those who have been ordained combined with so positive a view of sexuality is, I suspect, unprecedented in the documents of the Church. In 1967 Pope Paul VI issued his Encyclical Letter on priestly celibacy, *Sacerdotalis Caelibatus*. He acknowledged the changes in society and the way new questions had been raised about compulsory celibacy; he included elevated passages which can inspire us still; but there is nothing to compare with the raw appeal and urgency of John Paul II's declaration: man cannot live without love; his life is meaningless if he does not experience it intimately.

When we take this view seriously, however, we are doing more than simply adding a further element or dimension to our understanding of committed celibacy. We are causing a significant shift. Let me try to explain what I mean.

On my first visit to Los Angeles in 1986, my friends arranged for me to go on the tour of Universal Studios. I saw how E.T. could appear to be riding a bicycle over rooftops, the mechanized great white shark from *Jaws*, and the house made famous by Alfred Hitchcock's classic movie, *Psycho*, but that's the nearest I've been to a film set. I imagine that making movies is a complicated, demanding business, often a scene of creative disorder. Nevertheless, when a feature film is being made, a story is being told, there is a cast of characters, they have dialogue to speak, scenes are shot, the plot unfolds and comes to its conclusion. At least in that sense, all the elements are settled and under control. But sometimes something else happens. A famous example occurred in 1944 when Humphrey Bogart was making *To Have and Have Not*. His co-star was a young model-turned-actress, Lauren Bacall. They fell in love. They took care to be discreet about their affair, but for all their discretion their relationship became known. You only needed to see the rushes of a day's shoot to understand how. The chemistry between the actors had changed. A new dynamic element had been introduced, something that could not be controlled by the written scenes and script and plot.

Analogies are never perfect. All the same, I suggest that something similar is happening when the element of affective maturity, of human loving, is included in our understanding of celibacy. A teaching about celibacy based on the ideal of Jesus, on the relationship between the ordained and Christ, expressed in terms of the sacramental character of ordained ministry, and on celibacy as by law established is a teaching based on elements which can be controlled. They are static, idealized, abstract. To add affective maturity is not just to include an additional element; it is a different kind of element, something dynamic which forces us to review our understanding of celibacy afresh.

To put Pope John Paul's point in another way, if celibacy means we stop loving, it's not worth it. Many people have recognized that truth and looked for ways to express it. They sometimes talk of the perfect human whole as a realizing or reconciling of the masculine and feminine within each of us. In 1983, I came across an article which observed: '. . . for the celibate, there is still a need for a loving relationship with the opposite sex. This opposite sex can be a person, or it can be found within as the *anima* through meditation, dreams, active imagination, contemplative prayer and mystical experience, all of which are guides and means for the inward pilgrimage.'[4] There is much good sense in this article, but the language is abstract

4. Bernard J. Bush, 'Celibacy, Affectivity and Friendship', in *The Way Supplement*, no. 47 (1983), p. 74.

and removed from us. How are we in fact to be both loving and celibate? To many people the idea seems contradictory.

(iv)

Writing about living with compulsory celibacy in 1993, Jim O'Keefe who has since been President of Ushaw College, the seminary in the north-east of England, tells the story of how, as a newly ordained priest, he was answering a radio phone-in. One caller, he remembers, 'managed to put into words what many others were thinking when he asked: "I know you are a Catholic priest, but have you ever had sex with a girl in the back of your mini?" ' O'Keefe goes on:

> I seem to remember saying that I was indeed a priest, and I did drive a mini, but that I had never had sex with anyone in my life. The caller followed this up with a further question: 'Don't you think you're a bit odd then?' I then said something about knowing a fair number of people who talked about having a very active sex life, but there was little evidence that they were any less odd than I was.[5]

Sean Sammon, who is a clinical psychologist and, as I write in 2003, Superior General of the Marist Brothers, makes essentially the same point when he observes, 'Does it surprise you to learn that some of the most sexual people I know also live lives of celibate chastity? Spend time with any one of them, and you will be left with this lasting impression: here is a person who is deeply spiritual and profoundly human.'[6]

O'Keefe and Sammon are concerned with the same issue. There is more to being sexual than engaging in genital sexual intercourse. Contrary to the presumption in so much of Western culture, loving and being sexual are not to be identified with

5. James O'Keefe, 'Living with Compulsory Celibacy', in *The Way Supplement*, no. 77 (1993), p. 37.
6. Sean D. Sammon, 'Celibate Chastity: an Affair of the Heart', in *Priests and People* 15 (April 2001), p. 134.

physical activity. As some people have sex, but don't make love, so others, even without genital experience, can be loving and sexual. They are celibate. We are made for intimacy. To echo John Paul II again, human life is meaningless if a person does not experience and participate in love intimately. Intimacy here is much more than a euphemism for sexual intercourse. To be loving and celibate may be rare – although many more people are faithful to this life than may be supposed – but it is not abnormal. A love for Christ is decisive. 'The love of Christ overwhelms us' (2 Corinthians 5:14 Jerusalem Bible).

How is it to be explained? Only with difficulty. How do men and women find their lives overwhelmed by their love for someone who was executed brutally two thousand years ago? In 1998 Cardinal Godfried Danneels, Archbishop of Malines-Bruxelles, observed, 'I would say the why and wherefore of celibate love for Christ is celibate love for Christ. It cannot be explained further than that.'[7] I warm to that remark. In affairs of the heart explanations are not found easily. Feelings of love, emotions, are so memorable we can miss the fact that love is a matter of much more than emotion. It depends on decision. We love because we decide to. That is our choice. True love is based on commitment. Emotion is wonderful, especially when it keeps step with decision, but emotion of its nature is mercurial. We may love people completely, we may love the bones of them, and still at times feel thoroughly fed up with them, but deep-rooted decisions endure. Let me try to throw some light on what it means to be loving and celibate, to love by choice in a celibate way.

These decisions are not carried out perfectly all at once. They have to take root and grow. They need to be nurtured so that they can permeate our lives.[8] All loving is a matter of maturity, and maturity is not achieved instantly. Ripening takes time. I

7. Cardinal Godfried Danneels, 'Training Candidates for Priesthood', in *Origins* 28 (24 September 1998), p. 259.
8. See A.W. Richard Sipe, *Celibacy: A Way of Loving, Living, and Serving* (Dublin, 1996), p. 60.

remember one day a priest friend of mine saying with a smile, 'Have you ever noticed how we are always being told that we must grow in virtue? We have to grow in faith and hope and love, and prudence, and wisdom, and so on. But we are expected to be perfectly chaste immediately.' It comes as a relief to find Pope Paul VI acknowledging that chastity 'is not acquired all at once but results from a laborious conquest and daily affirmation' (*Sacerdotalis Caelibatus*, n. 73). To be loving and celibate is a struggle. It does not come easily. We do it, in Richard Sipe's words, 'deliberately, painfully, and slowly'.[9] Let's realize that first of all. It is not difficult to become discouraged. Let's return to Christ, to the person of Jesus.

(v)

The Gospels make it plain that Jesus was at ease among his companions: his disciples were his friends; when Lazarus died, he wept (see John 11:35); he was even invited into the homes of Pharisees. It is clear that people enjoyed his company and he enjoyed theirs.

It is also evident that he enjoyed the company of women. I have seen it suggested that he offers us an example of how to remain faithfully celibate by his custom of never being alone with a woman. The suggestion is based on his meeting with the Samaritan woman at the well. When the disciples returned, we are told that they marvelled that he was talking with a woman (see John 4:27). It is said to show that this solitary meeting was utterly exceptional. I find the suggestion extraordinary. They were more likely to have been surprised, as was the woman herself, because she was a Samaritan.

One of the most engaging aspects of the Jesus we meet in the Gospels is his ease with women, and not just the Bethany family of Martha and Mary. He befriends Mary of Magdala and is shown to be completely comfortable in his dealings with the

9. *ibid.*, p. 116.

woman taken in adultery. Indeed, when her accusers have retired, we are told that he is left alone with her (see John 8:9). He was also known to be a friend of prostitutes. If a friend, it is hard to suppose that he was not also rumoured to be a client as well. The rumours would have been false, but they indicate a man at ease in the company of women. When a woman breaks in while he is the guest at dinner of Simon the Pharisee, and weeps over his feet, drying them with her hair, kissing them and anointing them, he is unembarrassed and treats her with gentle kindness (see Luke 7:36–50). Jesus does not appear to have remained celibate by subjecting himself to iron self-discipline. The ease bears witness to maturity. He was not on his guard. He was comfortable with his companions and friends, the women as well as the men.

Friendship is invaluable. Moreover, in our society which tends to assume that close friendship is invariably sexually physical, the example of uncluttered friendship is reassuring. Friends, a good range of friends, are vital. Some people are shyer, more reserved; others will be extroverts: irrespective of temperament, we all need friends. Over the centuries there have been close and loving friendships between holy people who are celibate. Some are exceptional and have become well known: St Francis and St Clare, Jordan of Saxony and Blessed Diana D'Andalo, St Francis de Sales and St Jane Frances de Chantal. At the same time, these friendships are not to be seen merely as a way to compensate for something more intimate still. They are not pale imitations of marriage, substitutes for the celibate. Nor are they goals to be achieved of set purpose. It is not a question of every celibate going out in search of a Clare for his Francis, a Jordan for her Diana. They have their own integrity and they come as gift.

Friendship supplies the backcloth for our loving. If we are to fulfil the great commandment of love, we must be like Jesus, at ease in company, but ready also to love particular people, not just be loving in general.

Blood families come first. Although my father to whom I was close, died in 1976, my mother is still alive and well, and I have two sisters whose love for me has been an indispensable part of my life. They love me, but fortunately are not uncritical. Serious love will never be uncritical. One of life's most precious gifts is to know that you are loved and they give me that assurance. I love them in return and do not take them for granted.

All the same, our families ought to love us, as we should love them. And yet it is natural to hope for the love that is not the outcome of the family bond. We look for other loves. The family at Bethany suggests a model. We need our oases.

It would have been a rare weekend during my Oxford days when I didn't spend an evening with Frank and Mary Ashby in their home. Frank was the business administrator at the Catholic Chaplaincy. We first met in 1970. He was already a regular member of the University Pilgrimage to Lourdes and, when he retired in 1969, Michael Hollings persuaded him to move from Harrogate and support the way the Chaplaincy was developing. Frank and I always got on well, worked happily together, and quickly became good friends. He and Mary were wonderful to me and their family has become like an extension of my own. Frank died in 1992 and Mary is now in her nineties, but their children, scattered in different parts of the world, have always welcomed me to their homes. These are people I love.

Then there is another family. In 1978, although we had met only recently, they suggested that I should have the key to their home, so that, if I were ever passing and needed a break, even if I had been unable to warn them, I could call in and draw breath. I have often benefited from their kindness, not only in that way, but also by spending holidays with them, when I have been able to hide away, rest and relax. No price can be put on such generosity. Nor on the individual friendships that flourish, friendships of long-standing, even from schooldays, or from holidays, ships which are supposed to have passed in the night, but didn't, and have remained fundamental. All these friendships are invaluable and beyond compare. I acknowledge my immense good fortune. Not everyone will be as lucky. If I have been able to live my celibate life with a certain warmth and ease and approachability, then the credit is largely theirs; but these friendships are not substitutes for marriage. Nor do they make us immune. We may still fall in love.

What does it mean to be loving and sexual and celibate and in love? How are we to cope? The natural answer may point to commitment, but it is not a simple solution. To be committed to the life of ministerial priesthood is not a shield against falling in love, any more than is marriage for the married. Whatever our circumstances, new relationships can still surprise and confuse us. It is wonderful when commitment and emotion walk in step, but there are times when they seem determined to walk in opposite directions and tear us apart. What should we do?

(vi)

Many priests fall in love. They realize whom they would have wished to marry had they not been ordained. The recognition and acceptance of that love is an overwhelming, uplifting experience; it can be comforting, but also painful. To love deeply, but not to be able to give expression to that love and, moreover, to be always at a certain distance from the person you love, is costly. It is easy to identify with the sentiments expressed in a letter written during the Blitz in the Second World War, when a married couple were separated, which said, 'Sometimes in London I look up at a raw edge of masonry where a room has vanished from the other room, and I feel I know that loss and incompleteness as well as I know anything in life. I'm not a whole person alone, and the edge of the tear hurts all the time.'[10] I'm not a whole person alone. The cross we are asked to bear may seem unbearable. And yet the knowledge of that love can be a source of great strength, while, at the same time, it may also seem in some degree to qualify and lessen our love for God. These loves can look like rivals. The head may be able to

10. See Laurence Whistler, *The Initials in the Heart* (London, 1975), p. 173.

reconcile them, but the heart aches. I used to wonder and worry about it.

Then one summer during a retreat I was asked to use as a text for prayer that passage from the prophecy of Jeremiah where the prophet is sent to the potter's house and finds him working at his wheel. And Jeremiah reports that 'the vessel he was making of clay was spoiled in the potter's hand, and he reworked it into another vessel, as it seemed good to the potter to do.' I read it as a harsh text, this text about breaking. It made me wonder about my love for one particular person over many years. The love may have been chaste, but had she nevertheless meant too much to me? It was not a scruple. Had this love in fact absorbed too much of my time and attention? Had it in some way compromised my commitment to God? Should I not have been rather like the potter and broken it and reworked it? Yet to deny the goodness of that love seemed to me wrong. It was a hard and distressing moment. I wondered whether the particular grace of the retreat would be to discover the courage to make that break and end what I had so valued. But I could not see how that would be right. I felt bemused. Then I noticed the words which come next, 'O house of Israel, can I not do with you as this potter has done?', and I heard them, not as harsh words, requiring a break, but as gentle words, which inspire trust (see Jeremiah 18:1–6). And I knew that the Lord could do that, not break, but renew, rework. And I felt overcome with love and gratitude. I realized that, if I had in a way seen the two loves as rivals, I need do so no longer. I may still feel 'the edge of the tear', but have discovered how to live with it.

I am not suggesting that my conclusion is a solution for everyone. Each of us is unique. We handle these situations in different ways. All the same, it may perhaps indicate how someone, although celibate, may know what it means to love deeply and intimately and be faithful.

(vii)

To justify celibacy by scorning sexuality or by acclaiming it as the way to greater availability or more generous pastoral service is absurd. The power and the beauty of sexuality and the importance of intimate relationships, on the one hand, and the pastoral generosity of so many ordained people who are married, both in the Catholic tradition and in others, on the other, make nonsense of such arguments. Celibacy is not some calculated strategy for pastoral action. We are not celibate in order to be more available; we are rather more available because we are celibate. As Jim O'Keefe observed neatly: 'The availability flows from the fact of being celibate rather than being the cause of it.'[11]

The reason for celibate love for Christ is celibate love for Christ. Commitment is crucial. It is the great rock out of which the lives of those who have been ordained are carved. Our loving and sexuality, celibacy and fidelity are not additions attached to commitment, but are integral to it, the radical personal qualities which give it shape. And here too there is risk. The carving will not be without cost. It may crucify us. But we are prepared to accept the consequences because the love of Christ so overwhelms us that for us there is no alternative. We can do no other. The decision to follow him controls us. We have been called to spend our lives in sacrifice and service and we have accepted. We have chosen, in Herbert McCabe's arresting phrase, 'to be as possessed by love as he was'.[12] The emotion commonly may be mild, but the force of the commitment is irresistible. And sometimes something happens which takes us by surprise and stirs us.

In the Middle East the sun rises swiftly. It is spectacular. One morning some years ago, just before sunrise, I was sitting beside the Sea of Galilee reading Paul's letter to the Romans. I read his

11. O'Keefe, 'Living with Compulsory Celibacy', p. 41.
12. McCabe, *God Matters* (London, 1987), p. 219.

question, 'Who shall separate us from the love of Christ?' (Romans 8:35), and glanced up. At that very instant the sun appeared over the brow of the hills opposite and its reflection, a warm orange golden light, unrolled like a carpet and came racing across the surface of the lake to where I was sitting. The phenomenon, of course, was entirely natural, but the effect was breathtaking and unforgettable, a moment of comfort and grace.

7

Living and Praying

(i)

THE call to be both loving and celibate is a high risk for those who are ordained. It is easy to love, but we can get our loving wrong. Some of us fail and many experience failure. It is well documented. Failure, however, does not necessarily annul fidelity. We acknowledge weakness, seek forgiveness, and persevere afresh. We must not surrender, but we struggle on, strengthening our commitment and diving ever deeper. Reflecting sympathetically on these matters over many years, the psychiatrist Richard Sipe, once a Dominican but later a husband and father, has concluded: 'There is *no* possibility of participating seriously in the celibate process or any hope of achieving celibacy without a sound grounding in prayer.' He likens prayer for the celibate to air and water for us all.[1]

This reference to prayer is well judged. It is not offered as a placebo, as though prayer were blandly the solution to every difficulty. Sipe emphasizes well the importance of prayer for everyone, but what he has to say strikes special chords for those of us committed to celibacy. He describes prayer as 'the one place in time when we can be our real selves'. He explains the point disarmingly: 'There is a certain amount of deception and hypocrisy necessarily woven into the fabric of our daily lives . . . We have to make a "good impression" to carry on ordinary social interaction. Most of us, to one degree or another, even unconsciously, conduct our daily operation in ways that clue

1. A. W. Richard Sipe, *Celibacy: A Way of Loving, Living and Serving* (Dublin, 1996), p. 54.

others that we are competent, intelligent, trustworthy, emotionally stable, hold socially acceptable attitudes, and generally are successful. We have to posture.' Who cannot recognize what is being described here? There are games we people play in society. We posture. 'Prayer', however, he goes on, 'whatever the method, is the absence of posturing. Prayer means facing ourselves as we really are in the safety and privacy of our hearts.'[2]

When I first read this passage, it reminded me of a retreat I had made in 1971. I had been ordained about eighteen months earlier. In some ways my plan was over-ambitious. I went to stay at the Carmelite Monastery on Boars' Hill outside Oxford for a full eight days. I didn't ask for a director; I was revisiting materials gathered during my years as a seminarian. The days turned out to be long and I found them difficult, but I learnt one priceless lesson. By the third day, struggling in the midst of the silence and the hours of prayer, I realized that there was no hiding place. I had to face up to myself. Prayer is the absence of posturing.

And it is more than a matter of saying prayers.[3] All those who have been baptized are called to live lives of prayer, while once again those who are ordained are seen to have a particular responsibility. Our lives must be prayerful, sealed by prayerfulness. Nothing could be simpler, but we do not find it easy.

In 1978 Sister Wendy Beckett, renowned for her expertise on art, wrote an article for *The Clergy Review*. She called it 'Simple Prayer'. On the one occasion we met, a chance meeting in 1995, she told me it was quite unlike anything else she had ever been asked to write before or since. I think it is a masterpiece.[4] She anticipates Sipe. She describes prayer as 'the one place in all the world where there is nowhere to hide'. Prayer is the absence of posturing. And what is it positively? 'The essential act of prayer', she says, 'is to stand unprotected before God.' Then she asks,

2. *ibid.*, pp. 54–5.
3. See Roderick Strange, *Living Catholicism* (London, 2001), pp. 11–26.
4. Wendy Mary Beckett, 'Simple Prayer', *The Clergy Review* lxiii (February, 1978), pp. 42–5.

'What will God do?' And at once she supplies the answer: 'He will take possession of us.'

But how can we manage to stand in that way, unprotected before God? Once again, the answer is simple, but not easy. The answer is desire. 'Prayer is prayer', Wendy Beckett writes, 'if we want it to be.' What is it we desire? What do we truly long for? She goes on: 'Ask yourself: What do I really want when I pray? Do you want to be possessed by God? Or, to put the question more honestly, do you want to want it?' It is a humane, revealing question. Challenged by the question, forced to say whether or not I want to be possessed by God, I might well reply, almost under my breath, that perhaps I don't; but I might also add, 'I wish I did.' That is enough. Do you want to want it? she asks.

> Then you have it. The one point Jesus stressed and repeated and brought up again is that: 'Whatever you ask the Father, he will grant it you'. . . . When you set yourself down to pray, *what do you want*? If you want God to take possession of you, then you are praying. That is all prayer is. There are no secrets, no shortcuts, no methods. Prayer is the utterly ruthless test of your sincerity.

This is the point at which she describes it as 'the one place in all the world where there is nowhere to hide'.[5]

What do you want? What do you long for? What do you desire? To hear those questions should, I hope, strike chords. We have just been wondering about what it means to be both loving and celibate. We applauded the part played by emotion; feelings are not to be despised; but we acknowledged above all the importance of decision: 'We love because we decide to . . . True love is based on commitment.'[6] This decision is not driven by emotion; behaviour is not controlled by feeling; it follows from desire. To love and yet be faithfully celibate is a decision which reveals who we are and who we want to be, not simply

5. *ibid.*, p. 43.
6. See above, p. 80.

how we feel. We make a commitment. It touches the very depths of our personality. For those who run the risk of discipleship, commitment is crucial. We recognize that we have to be ready to run the risk, to accept the consequences of our commitment, because we have passed beyond calculation. We are not trying to be priests on our own terms. We are governed by desire, not by feeling. We run the risk of discipleship because of our desire to come close to God: we follow the undertow rather than the surf, we are led where we do not wish to go, we accept the invitation to be square pegs in round holes.[7] Prayer too, like our commitment to loving celibacy and our carrying the cross, has to be governed by desire. If we are to be prayerful people, it does not depend on how we feel. Desire is the key.

That may be all well and good, but what will this kind of praying be like? It is easy to acknowledge the importance of prayer and prayerfulness in principle, but how can it be made real in practice?

(ii)

Let's begin by stating the obvious: prayer nurtures our relationship with God. And, because of that, it is not only something we do. The relationship is mutual. God is not a lofty monarch whose attention we are trying to attract by the originality of our thoughts and the eloquence of our words. God is involved. He takes the initiative. Our desire to come close to God 'arises from the depths of God's desire for us'. In a powerful and memorable image, inspired by St Augustine, 'prayer is the encounter of God's thirst with ours. God thirsts that we may thirst for him' (see *Catechism of the Catholic Church*, n. 2560). Desire is the bedrock of prayer: his longing for us and our longing for him. And, to repeat it once more, it is not merely a matter of saying prayers; we must become prayerful. What does that mean? Writing to the Thessalonians, Paul tells them to pray constantly

7. See above, p. 32.

(see 1 Thessalonians 5:17), and that may give us a clue. He can't be referring to a ceaseless recitation of formal prayers. Over the years I have found a number of images instructive.

First of all, I think of prayer as a foreign language. At the same time I need to remember that we use images for what they can teach us; we don't have to squeeze significance from every detail. In this case, the weakness of the image lies in the reference to language. It may keep us concentrating on the *saying* of prayers, but that would be a distraction here. The value of the image lies in the reference to the language being foreign. What is foreign is almost by definition unfamiliar, and prayer is a foreign language because it doesn't come to us naturally. It is unfamiliar. But those who live abroad, for example, have to persevere. Gradually they come to speak the language of their adopted country better. Some are so gifted that in time they speak it like a native, while even for those less gifted, if they will persevere, it can become as natural a means for communicating as their mother tongue. But two activities are necessary. First, there are particular lessons to be learnt, like vocabulary, grammar, syntax, idioms, and turns of phrase, but it mustn't end there. We learn for a purpose: there is the need for regular and frequent conversation so as to come to speak it quite naturally. An occasional enthusiastic blitz will be of little use.

Secondly, I think of prayer as being like playing a musical instrument. Except perhaps for a rare genius, playing an instrument does not come to us naturally either. Once again, two activities are needed. First, like learning the details of a language, it is necessary to become thoroughly familiar with the piano or violin or trumpet, whatever the instrument happens to be, and to practise it, and rehearse; but, second, all that familiarity, practice and rehearsal will count for little, if taken no further: there needs also to be performance.

Learning a language and playing an instrument may both be taken as images for prayerfulness. The first teaches us that what begins as foreign and unfamiliar can become native and natural to us, if we use it regularly and frequently, while the second shows us that our purpose is not confined to the time set aside for practice and rehearsal, but leads to performance: we pray to become prayerful. That must be our disposition.

But prayer will not usually become natural, nor will our lives become prayerful, unless some special time is also set aside. Some practice, some time for rehearsal, seems to be essential. And more than that. Such time is not to be given grudgingly. We need a third image. Times of prayer are not just to be compared with learning vocabulary and practising scales. Prayer is also like our experience of loving. When we love, we do not spend every waking moment thinking about the beloved. At the start, when we first fall in love, we may – it will be one of the signs that we are smitten – but loving is not obsessive like that. On the other hand, we delight in the time which can be reserved exclusively for the one we love. To claim to love deeply, but to have no desire to spend any time with the beloved would be strange indeed. While prayerfulness must come to permeate our lives, there need to be times as well which we devote exclusively to God. And this, of course, is precisely what we often find most difficult. Nor are we alone in that. What a relief to discover that Thérèse of Lisieux had a tendency to go to sleep in times of formal prayer.[8]

There are many ways of praying. Libraries have been written on different schools of spirituality. The advice of Dom John Chapman, 'Pray as you can and do not try to pray as you can't', remains invaluable.[9] When it comes to praying, nothing can be dictated or forced, but I want to offer one suggestion. It won't suit everyone. Even if it did, it wouldn't suit everyone all the time. If it helps you now, you may have to change it later. I have come to value it greatly, but I know that in the future I will probably have to change it too. That's all right. For the present, it is serving me well.

8. See Simon Tugwell OP, *Ways of Imperfection: an Exploration of Christian Spirituality* (London, 1984), p. 223.
9. John Chapman, *Spiritual Letters* (London, 1959), p. 109.

(iii)

In the Fourth Gospel, we are told that Jesus, shortly after raising Lazarus from the dead, went back to his Bethany home. Lazarus was there, with his sisters, Martha and Mary. During the meal Mary came in with costly ointment, pure nard. Nard was an ointment used for healing; it was very expensive; its smell was enchanting. She poured it over Jesus' feet and then wiped his feet with her hair. Judas protested that the gesture was wasteful. He asked why the ointment had not been sold for three hundred denarii and the money given to the poor. John's Gospel explains this protest by reminding us that he was a thief and the one who betrayed Jesus (see John 12:1–6). We don't need to bother with that. It's instructive to see the incident from a different angle.

In principle it is natural to deplore waste; wasteful behaviour is indefensible. Then again, it may offer us a means of escape. Sometimes we need to spend, but to spend may be costly and demanding. What a relief if we can identify that spending as waste and avoid it. But the solution may not be so simple. In our context, when we think about praying, we have to spend time, and that too is demanding. How convenient if we could judge that time as wasted and not bother. But Jesus in Bethany is teaching us a different lesson: we are allowed to be extravagant to those we love. Tony Philpot, priest, writer, and experienced spiritual director, has caught the point perfectly. He asks what this nard is for us. And he answers: 'My equivalent of costly ointment is time.' Nard is time; time is nard. We are loathe to waste it. And so he explains, 'In the modern world, time is the most valuable thing I have. To give it freely to Our Lord is the greatest compliment I can pay him.'[10] So let us begin there, whatever our temperament, extrovert or introvert, active or passive, social or reserved. We need to give the Lord time. Some of the busiest people I know still find time to jog daily or work out in a gym several times a week. They don't begrudge it. They

10. Tony Philpot, *You Shall Be Holy* (Buxhall, 2003), p. 30.

argue, of course, that they need to keep fit physically in order to work effectively, and they are right; but for the same reason we need to keep fit spiritually. That too takes time. However busy we may be, we can always find time for what matters to us. We must find time for prayer. The crucial question asks how that time is to be spent. We wonder what we ought to be doing.

(iv)

'Late have I loved you, beauty so old and so new: late have I loved you.' Augustine's words at the climax of his *Confessions* are well known. Then at once he continued: 'And see, you were within and I was in the external world and sought you there . . . You were with me, and I was not with you.'[11] Here may be the vital clue for us as well. Our situation may not be as dramatic as Augustine's, but the essential pattern may be the same. When we try to pray, we often wonder what we should do and go looking for it, when in fact we need only to attend to the presence within: 'You were with me.' We must attend to the presence, savour the presence, enjoy it. In conversation one day Tony Philpot suggested to me that we should see ourselves as 'tabernacles': the Lord is within. I found the idea immensely helpful. We carve out some time, find, if possible, a quiet place, although that may not be necessary, because the presence may absorb us even in a noisy crowd, and attend to that presence within. We try to keep our attention focused and alert.[12]

There are many ways of doing that. People write about the use of a mantra. I wouldn't presume to offer anything so technical and I find my own attention can be held in different ways at different times. There is no single word or phrase which carries me automatically into prayer. The most important part is wanting to be there, the desire to enjoy the presence. And then it can

11. Augustine, *Confessions* X, xxvii (38), p. 201.

12. Those who want to pursue this method more precisely might be helped by reading M. Basil Pennington OCSO, *Centering Prayer* (New York, 2001).

help to repeat the name 'Jesus', or a phrase, 'My Lord and my God' or 'Lord, I believe; help my unbelief'. Images too can serve the same purpose, like the potter's jar, which I mentioned earlier, or the mustard seed. It is not a question of working out ideas, but of an image, rich with associations, helping to keep the attention in tune with the presence. Sometimes a Gospel passage can help in the same way. Preparing a homily or a more discursive reflection may have made an impact. The memory remains. A particular favourite of mine is the scene from St Matthew's Gospel where Jesus walks on the water and invites Peter to come to him (see Matthew 14:25–33).

In 1993, while I was on retreat, I was asked to use this passage to prompt my prayer. I was to make Peter's words my own: 'Lord, if it is you, bid me come to you on the water', and to open myself to the reply, 'Come'.

Peter, we are told, got out of the boat and walked towards Jesus. Paintings of the scene tend to show him on his way to Jesus, but losing confidence and beginning to sink. Jesus reaches forward and holds him up. That captures well the sense of the Greek text, but the English translation I was using said simply that Peter 'came to Jesus'. That can, of course, mean that Peter was coming 'towards Jesus', as a later edition put it more explicitly. But that particular expression suggested to me that Peter began to sink, not on his way to Jesus, but when he was already there. I had an image of him striding confidently across the lake, greeting his friend, and only then, as he looks about, does the enormity of what he has done strike him. Then he starts to sink and feels the hand supporting his elbow and hears the voice in his ear, 'O man of little faith, why did you doubt?'

The image of journeying has been in vogue for decades. We are all on pilgrimage, but have not yet arrived. Applying this passage to myself on retreat, thirty years after beginning my studies for the priesthood, I thought of the way I had in some real sense 'come to Jesus', my commitment was made, I was standing beside him, he was standing beside me. And so now, years later, recalling that scene and the Gospel phrase that Peter 'came to Jesus' can help me remain attentive to the presence within. I could suggest other examples. You can supply your own.

Living and praying we need time and attention, gazing on the Beloved. As Wendy Beckett noted, it is simple, but not easy. And we may worry that we are in fact deceiving ourselves, passing off as prayer what is in fact no more than blankness and time-wasting. When we are tired, sleepy, and distracted, it can easily seem like that. Is there any way of checking what we are doing? I believe there is. I wish I knew the Spanish mystics better than I do, but one part of *The Ascent of Mount Carmel* by St John of the Cross seems to me especially valuable here.[13]

(v)

At one stage John is discussing the signs which indicate a person's readiness for this kind of quiet prayer. He is actually speaking of a definite move from discursive meditation to contemplation. That definite move may be precisely what some people experience, but many others, I suspect, who may not be aware of that particular grace, nevertheless feel sometimes the tug to contemplation when they pray. It is, so to speak, part of their spiritual diet. In fact, those who are ordained, cannot settle for contemplation alone. We must wander abroad: we have to pray the Divine Office, celebrate liturgy, recite the rosary, and must not simply study the Scriptures in order to preach, but have to explore them in prayer. All the same, we may feel a call to be quiet, to gaze on the Beloved. How can we know that all is well?

St John says there are three signs. Firstly, in those periods at least when we long for quiet, we realize that we are no longer able to remain in a prayer which is governed by reasoning and

13. John of the Cross, *The Ascent of Mount Carmel*, II, xiii, in *The Complete Works of John of the Cross*, Vol. I, translated and edited by E. Allison Peers (Wheathampstead, 1974), pp. 108–11.

the imagination. Secondly, we find we have no desire to fix our attention on any other particular object instead. And thirdly, we are pleased to be alone and waiting 'with loving attentiveness upon God . . . in inward peace and quietness and rest', without any further meditating, reasoning, or intellectual exploration. And all three signs are necessary. The first without the second, John observes, could be caused by distraction or lack of commitment. We can no longer reflect or use our imagination in prayer, because we are preoccupied with something else. But in our own praying there must be no alternative. We find we have moved on from that kind of reasoning and use of the imagination altogether. We are at rest and open. However, the third element is needed as well. The first and second are not sufficient without it. The lack of focused prayerful reflection and a mind open but unfilled could be caused by melancholy or depression, idleness or day-dreaming. We must also be fixed with loving attention on the Beloved. We are guided purely by that longing and desire. When we can detect all three of these signs, we can move into that inner silence with confidence.

(vi)

There is no easy recipe for prayer. However, to live the Christian life and to live it faithfully with the expectations which ministerial priesthood lays upon us makes prayer indispensable. It can be difficult and dry. Michael Hollings used to say that prayer is like an addiction, but the hangover comes first. Once we acquire the taste, it is hard to give up, but it can be so difficult to begin. We have to persevere. When Michael was studying for the priesthood in Rome, he used often to go out for a walk after lunch instead of taking a siesta. He found a church that had exposition and remained open all afternoon. He has described his experience: 'There I often literally sweated it out, in dull, dumb, boring, knee-aching slog. I slept there often; I seldom had much sense of prayer. Yet I went back there again and again, day by day, like a drowning man grabbing at a lifeline.'[14] Not everyone will do that or be able to do it. It is easy to ask what the point of it can be. And yet Michael became one of the great masters of his day in England, guiding people into depths of prayerfulness which they had never at first even imagined.

When we give ourselves faithfully to praying, we sow seed, or more accurately we find that the Lord is sowing seed in us which at the time probably falls unfelt into our hearts. The labour may be hard and disappointing, the hours long, the distractions relentless. We wonder what can come of it. But if we remain faithful, we find that there is a harvest. Somehow people are helped, responsibilities are carried out, homilies are preached, crises are suffered but survived. The link may not be visible, but what has been sown faithfully in spite of tedium, is bearing fruit. The abundance of the harvest takes our breath away.

14. Michael Hollings, *Living Priesthood* (Great Wakering, 1977), p. 21.

8

Accounting for our Hope

(i)

STIRRING words in the First Letter of Peter offer an invitation and issue a command: 'in your hearts reverence Christ as Lord. Always be prepared to make a defence to any one who calls you to account for the hope that is in you' (1 Peter 3:15). The invitation is offered and the command issued to all the baptized. Once again, we are not in an area reserved exclusively for those who have been ordained; we have only to think of the legions of dedicated catechists and professional lay theologians whose commitment and studies have graced the Church, not to mention the parents without number who have been the first teachers of their children in the ways of faith. Nor is this account a matter for formal teaching alone. In words made famous in his reflections on evangelization, Pope Paul VI declared, 'Modern man listens more willingly to witnesses than to teachers, and if he does listen to teachers, it is because they are witnesses' (*Evangelii Nuntiandi*, n. 41). Once again, our lives must be living gospel. All the same, there is a message to be proclaimed as well, there are lessons to be taught. The call to account for our hope places a specific obligation on the ordained. Here too, what parents and catechists and lay theologians may indeed do with wonderful skill is expected of priests. Integral to the vocation of the ordained is a summons to account for the hope that is in us.

One friend of mine who has been a parish priest for many years, spends an hour each day after breakfast reading theology. Some days he can't. There may be a requiem to celebrate or a diocesan meeting to attend or an unexpected visitor, an inevitable aspect of every priest's life, but his normal routine includes an hour daily for serious reading and study. He gives it priority. It is so easy to regard study as extra, something to be fitted in when there is nothing else to do. But there is always something else to do. We need to set time aside for study as carefully as we set it aside for prayer. It isn't a luxury for those who have been ordained. We are not being self-indulgent. It is a duty. It will appeal to some more than others, but it is in fact as necessary as exercise for the body and prayer for the spirit. It is particularly important at present. Let me suggest why.

First, to be blunt, there is a general indifference to what we have to say. Some people are just ignorant. They are like Jessica, a character in Iris Murdoch's novel, *The Nice and the Good*, who, we are told, 'was . . . entirely outside Christianity. Not only had she never believed or worshipped, she had never been informed about the Bible stories in her home or school. Christ was a figure in a mythology, and she knew about as much about him as she knew about Apollo. She was in fact an untainted pagan . . .'.[1] Christianity can make no sense to Jessica, not because it is meaningless, but because she lacks the means to make sense of it. Others don't care. Many have simply lost interest. They may yearn for the spiritual, but they reject the institutional Church and its message. There are others, however, who may not be indifferent. They may be actively hostile. As rector of a seminary preparing men to work in various parts of the world, including, for example, India, Nigeria, and Russia, I am well aware that they may have to confront that hostility. Then again, especially in Western Europe, in Australia, and in North America, there is a prevailing viewpoint which no longer believes that human reason has in any case the capacity to uncover truth which is both objective and universal. The French have an expression, 'tolérance morale': everything is relative; simply take the train standing at your local station to whatever destination it takes you; that will be fine; it makes no difference which train you get on. And finally, there are the problems and questions which

1. Iris Murdoch, *The Nice and the Good* (London, 1969), p. 83.

arise in the light of fresh scientific discoveries and further developments in technology and which are said to cast doubt on Christian teaching.

It's a bleak picture: no one is interested in what we have to say; they are either ignorant, indifferent, or actively hostile; they don't believe any conclusion will have objective value in any case, and whatever new knowledge is emerging they regard as speaking against the gospel, not in its favour. And underlying this position is a viewpoint perhaps best characterized as fragmentation.

The coherence which people used to champion has been lost, it has been broken into pieces. In fact confidence in the very possibility of coherence which gives meaning to experience and understanding has been undermined. It is like watching a film in which you are always unsure whether what you are being shown is the main narrative, a dream sequence, or the way events are being perceived by one or other of the characters. Is this a parable for the human condition? Is there a main narrative at all, or are all our lives in fact like dream sequences, or locked exclusively within each individual's way of perceiving? This lack of coherence, this fragmentation, is seen as the distinguishing mark of that postmodernism which seems to be resolutely hostile to religious faith and commitment. We should not be under any illusions about the scale of the task facing those who are called to proclaim the gospel, and especially those upon whom that responsibility is laid directly. And let me tighten the screw a little further.

We must never forget the incarnation. Pope Paul VI once declared: 'Christ became the contemporary of some men and spoke their language. Our faithfulness to him demands that this contemporaneousness should be maintained' (see *Pastores Dabo Vobis*, n. 52). How can we maintain it? How are we to proclaim the gospel of Christ in today's society when its culture is characterized by indifference, subjectivity, relativism, and fragmentation? The language of such a culture seems to be one in which the gospel simply cannot be expressed. Culture and gospel seem to be opposed to each other. How can we account for the hope that is in us in this setting?

(ii)

Some people may be in thrall to relativism and subjectivism, but there is no need for everyone to succumb. Our minds instinctively seek out knowledge and try to establish what is true. Sometimes our conclusions may indeed be relative and subjective, but to hold that our grasp of knowledge and truth can only ever be like that, that what we come to know and hold as true can never be objective as well, would reduce intellectual activity to little more than a trivial pursuit. We can do better than that. And even Pope John Paul II has remarked that postmodernism has sometimes been judged positively as well as negatively and has referred to it as meriting 'appropriate attention' (*Fides et Ratio*, n. 91).

Those who wish to give it that attention might start by reading Michael Paul Gallagher's book, *Clashing Symbols*.[2] For our purposes it may be enough to notice the distinction he makes between postmodernism and postmodernity. 'Where postmodernism tends to express itself in a series of nihilist doubts about "modern" claims,' he writes, 'cultural postmodernity can be seen as an attempt to purify the modern inheritance.'[3] In other words, it tempers modernity's more arrogant claims by offering a fresh perspective.

Postmodernism and postmodernity may have qualities in common and postmodernity has its shadow side as well, but, as Gallagher explains, it may also point to something more positive, imaginative, and hopeful. Where most commentators see the fragmentation and loss of coherence which characterize postmodernity as handicapping the proclamation of the gospel, he

2. Michael Paul Gallagher, *Clashing Symbols: an Introduction to Faith and Culture*; revised edition (London, 2003), pp. 98–114.
3. *ibid.*, p. 91.

finds a potential ally. The risk of discipleship may take us against the tide, as we have often noticed, or, to use Gallagher's metaphor, postmodernity may seem to lead us into a cultural desert where the 'landscape seems even more a formula for paralysis'. Nevertheless, he argues, the new cultural desolation may whet the spiritual appetite. The hunger is stronger. And in spite of the danger that this spirituality may float free, lacking the definiteness which is characteristic of Christian faith, it has all the same 'a significantly new tone of religious openness'.[4] All is not lost. We must return to the original question: how are we to offer an account of the hope that is in us?

(iii)

Wrestling with that question, may I suggest first of all what we must not do? We must not become negative and defensive. It is true that the Letter of Peter urges us to 'be prepared to make a *defence*' to anyone who calls us to account for the hope that is in us, but I don't think it is referring to battlements and fortresses. The tone is one of encouragement and the emphasis is on our *being prepared*. That means we have to be clear thinking. In spite of the suspicion of coherence which we have already noticed, when people ask questions, they usually like to be given clear answers. I remember reading a book review years ago by Frederick Copleston, the Jesuit historian of philosophy, where he observed wryly that the book would not appeal to those who regarded obscurity as a mark of scholarship. Obscurity is not a mark of scholarship. As pastoral priests, giving an account of the hope that is in us, we must prize clarity. And clarity is more likely to shine through when we maintain an interest in the matters which should be of concern to us and throw ourselves into our study of them with enthusiasm. Then we acquire a taste for them.

One result of being prepared, of clear thinking, and of being

4. *ibid.*, pp. 87, 95–6.

enthusiastic about study will be to acquire a cast of mind which has the confidence to explore more deeply the faith we hold dear. We must recognize what that implies. Years ago, Raymond Brown mapped out various approaches to contemporary Scripture studies and Christology.[5] I suggest that what he says is capable of far wider application.

Surveying the scene, it is possible to identify extreme positions, both conservative and liberal, which champion their views sincerely and with passion, but which are not scholarly. Their extremism and lack of scholarship – in spite at times of outward scholarly embellishment – are made evident by their inability to engage constructively in a conversation with those who hold views different from their own. Perhaps their passion blinds them. They make debate a waste of time. At the same time, however, there is a range of other people whose views may be categorized as more or less liberal or conservative, but who, while no less passionate, will engage gladly in debate in pursuit of learning and deeper understanding. It is not necessary to canonize one single standpoint within this range. Indeed, a person may quite consistently be more conservative in handling some issues, more liberal in handling others. What is indispensable, however, if we are to give an account of our hope, is that we remain open to new discoveries. We engage in the conversation. Firm in faith, we maintain a sense of the richness of the truth we are exploring. The richness can be illustrated in many ways, not only in propositions. It can be illustrated in art.

For the Jubilee in the year 2000, there was an exhibition in London called *Seeing Salvation*. It was outstanding. Vast numbers came to visit it. It had gathered together from many places images of Jesus, the child with his Mother, the Good Shepherd, Jesus in his passion, Jesus crucified, Jesus being taken down from the cross, Jesus risen from the dead and confronting his disciples,

5. See Raymond E. Brown, ' "Who Do Men Say That I Am?" – A Survey of Modern Scholarship on Gospel Christology', in *Biblical Reflections on Crises Facing the Church* (London, 1975), pp. 20–37.

Holman Hunt's Jesus as the Light of the World, Francisco de Zurbaran's startling image of the Bound Lamb, and many, many others. These images were wonderfully varied. Were some of them true and others false? Even if we concentrated simply on Jesus in his passion, we found there were images from different centuries, different cultures and countries, and different traditions. But how could we say that any were false? For all their variety, all were true. Truth is not monolithic. It can show itself in different ways. That is what helps to make learning a delight. New insights open up before us. As we engage in study, we become more capable of accounting for the hope that is in us. But it makes demands on us.

(iv)

Ministerial priesthood summons us to human maturity, to committed spirituality, and to a care for those whom we are asked to serve. But that is not the whole story. We are asked to make the faith our own and for a purpose: we must be able as well to communicate it effectively to those who come to us, because they are searching. Some come, sharing our faith and wanting to take hold of it more deeply and firmly, others, perhaps from different Christian traditions, come with questions. Then there are still others who come, who do not share our faith; they may believe, but they are not Christians. Others again may have no religious faith at all, but they are keen to talk. What kind of conversation can we have with them? The dialogue has to be genuine. How do we prepare ourselves to talk to those who are essentially at one with us, and to those as well who have different views, but who are crying out for a serious conversation? These are far-reaching questions. In the first instance, it may help to notice the way we handle sacred Scripture, and, in the second, how we should take part in dialogue.

1. *The Scriptures*

How are we to interpret the Scriptures? It is a responsibility laid upon us. We have to preach Sunday after Sunday, year after year, often to the same people. How are we to open these texts up for them?

Through our studies we learn the importance of interpreting texts by placing them in their historical context and by appraising them critically. We recognize, for example, the different nuances and emphases which characterize the Gospels: in Matthew, the five great discourses, in Mark, the centrality of the Christological question, 'Who do men say the Son of man is?', in Luke, the road to and then away from Jerusalem, and in John, the great signs. When we are preaching, whether on a Sunday or during the week, it will be natural sometimes to allude to those distinguishing features. Again, when quoting the words of Jesus, while we may often do so without qualification, there can also be occasions when we indicate variations from Gospel to Gospel: only Matthew has a sermon on the Mount in which Jesus exclaims, 'Blessed are the poor in spirit'; the parallel discourse in Luke takes place on the plain and the exclamation is starker, 'Blessed are the poor'. What might that difference be telling us? Then consider the seven words of Jesus on the cross. Do they occur in every Gospel? No. The cry of desolation, 'My God, my God, why hast thou forsaken me?' occurs only in the earliest tradition, in Mark and Matthew (Mark 15:34//Matthew 27:46); only in Luke do we find the gentler sayings, 'Father, forgive them; for they know not what they do' (23:34), 'Today you will be with me in paradise' (23:43), and, 'Father, into thy hands I commit my spirit' (23:46); while in John there is majesty and control: 'Woman, behold, your son! . . . Behold, your mother!' (19:26, 27), 'I thirst' (19:28), and 'It is finished' (19:30). There is a development in the accounts of the passion, from agony to control. What can we learn from that? By being sensitive ourselves to the sacred texts, pointing out these differences almost in passing, we can help people raise their awareness of what our Scriptures are teaching us.

Nor is that everything. We can help them value even more the texts they already love. For example, when a parish group is meeting, perhaps for catechesis, or to reflect on issues related to justice and peace, or to plan some event, we can arrange an evening when its members may be invited to come with a particular favourite biblical passage or quotation. They are then given the opportunity to introduce what they have chosen and explain its significance. As a rector, I have held such sessions with students who were to receive shortly afterwards the ministry of Reader. It is a lay ministry, but a first formal step on the way to ordination. As its title indicates, those who receive this ministry are being drawn into a special love of and care for the Scriptures, so this kind of meeting is particularly appropriate. They have always been memorable occasions which have enriched those present, because, whatever the level of academic expertise, they show how personal ideas also have their place. Just as there is more to music than the notes – there must be performance to bring it to life – so there is more to our Scriptures than academic analyses can convey: the historico-critical method is good, but incomplete without *lectio divina*, the way each one of us reads these texts. This book has already made use of some of my favourite texts, for example, Peter walking on water and coming to Jesus, and the potter's jar in Jeremiah which was reworked and renewed. How important it is for us to have the confidence and the understanding to help people be nourished by the word in that way, to make the word personal, to make it come alive.

2. *Dogma and Dialogue*

In January 2002 I had the good fortune to attend a Conference in Rome on Inculturation and Inter-Religious Dialogue, which had been planned by the Cardinal Suenens Center of John Carroll University in Cleveland, Ohio. It articulated some key difficult questions and forced the participants to face them. They are questions for everyone, but questions too which those engaged in pastoral ministry are forced to confront. We are drawn into relationships with those we are asked to serve, not just Catholic parishioners and Christians of other traditions who share our desire for unity, but our partners in inter-religious dialogue as well. Indeed, the issues surrounding dialogue arise most sharply in our conversations with them. What should the nature of those conversations be? It may be helpful to review the situation. How are we to proceed with integrity?

Catholic Christianity is a dogmatic religion. We believe that there is only one God and yet that this one God is three Persons, Father and Son and Holy Spirit. And we believe that, as there is only this one God, then our God is the one true God. There is no other. We must have no truck with other gods. By definition they must be false. How, then, am I as a Christian to understand the faith of those who believe in God, but who do not believe in God as I do? Does my Christian faith require me to consider their belief false? Beneath a cover of courtesy, do I think of them as worshipping idols? Is dialogue merely camouflage for proselytism? Am I listening sincerely in order to learn, or is it merely a way of making other people lower their guard, so as to manoeuvre them into agreement with me? And if, on the other hand, I can acknowledge their faith as true, dismissing as beneath contempt the very idea of idol worship, then am I left in a quagmire of indifferentism?

In our ministry we need to be aware of these issues. Inter-religious dialogue can no longer be optional for us. We have got to take part, both as servants of the truth and because the threat of conflict in our world is more intense than ever. But how are we to proceed?

Religious commitment can easily be made the scapegoat for violence. We have to remember that God is not to be identified exclusively with any one religious tradition. Some people may find that shocking and I am not suggesting that everything which is called a religious experience will be authentic in fact. But to acknowledge that religious experience may be found elsewhere is not to drift into indifferentism. It is no part of Christian faith that all authentic religious experience is confined to Christianity alone. On the contrary, as the Second Vatican Council declared, the Catholic Church 'rejects nothing of what is true and holy' in other religions, but holds in high regard whatever they contain which reflects 'a ray of that truth' which enlightens everyone (*Nostra Aetate*, n. 2). And we need to recognize what that implies.

If genuine religious experience is always ultimately experience of God and if authentic religious experience is to be acknowledged amongst those who are not Christians, amongst Jews and Muslims and Buddhists and Hindus and others, then that experience, because it is authentic, can only be experience of the one true God. There is no other God to authenticate it. We must do more than respect the good that can be discerned in other faiths; wherever we find genuine religious faith we must acknowledge the divine presence.

To recognize God's presence elsewhere, however, should not make us indifferent to the way we recognize his presence among us. Christians affirm the unique nature of the revelation which has come through Jesus Christ. Remember again the exhibition, *Seeing Salvation*. Many a picture may capture its subject truly without being a masterpiece. We do not need to reject as false the genuinely religious convictions that other people hold dear. We should respect them profoundly. But we prize our own, the understanding we have of Christ, as the masterpiece. The uniqueness of Christ does not lie in his being the only revelation of God's truth, but in his being, as we believe, its supreme and definitive revelation. The drama of salvation is a drama of reconciliation.[6]

The Father who has created us acted out of love. We exist because we are loved. Created as free beings, however, we were not forced to love in return; we were able to reject that love and we did; that rejection is sin. But God loved the world so much that he sent his only Son to proclaim that love afresh by

6. See above, p. 25.

the way he lived, by the teaching he gave, and finally by the death he died on the cross: 'God shows his love for us in that while we were yet sinners Christ died for us' (Romans 5:8). The love of God is revealed by that death. Nor did matters end there. For the Father raised Jesus from the dead and sent into our midst the Holy Spirit. The Spirit has not come as a substitute, to compensate for Jesus' absence, but rather to make him present more intimately than ever. Confronted by such overwhelming love, we are called to repent and turn back in love. We are invited to be reconciled not only to God, but also to one another. When the risen Jesus greeted his disciples, he said to them, 'Peace be with you' (John 20:19, 26), and instructed them to be instruments of forgiveness. We are caught up in the reconciliation which Jesus proclaimed.

We can recognize God's presence among others, but we nurture his presence among us and approach them, not deceitfully, but inspired by the spirit of reconciliation. We hope that they may want to share what we have by the way we account for the hope that is in us.

(v)

These issues are real and urgent. Making the Scriptures come alive and engaging in genuine, respectful conversation and dialogue lie at the heart of our ministry. Recognizing these questions can touch us humanly and stir us spiritually, but it needs also to encourage us intellectually to be well prepared for our ministry, not by polishing up a neat set of 'answers', which will answer nothing, but by helping us acquire a mental outlook attuned to the actual demands which will be made of us.

That outlook will not happen by chance. It requires serious, steady, committed, hard work. No one should underestimate the enormity of the task. It won't be enough to remain with what we find personally comfortable. In spite of its joys and the satisfaction it can bring, study is a risky business. St Thomas Aquinas associated the beatitude, 'Blessed are those who mourn', with intellectuals because, when they seek and find new truth, they can be like people bereaved because they have to abandon the earlier formulations of truth which until that time they had cherished.[7] Here once more we are faced with the risk of discipleship. We sometimes discover things which we would rather not know. It calls for significant adjustments in our ways of thinking. That can be painful.

It reminds me of a remark made by Jim O'Keefe when he was addressing the National Conference of Priests of England and Wales in 1997. He had been talking about change and how difficult we find it, and he offered a simple poignant example. He drew our attention to the fact that the four Gospels had come down to us in Greek, not in the Aramaic which Jesus had spoken. And then he observed: 'I wonder if it was a hugely painful decision for the early Church to use the language of the people to be evangelised, rather than the language of the Sermon on the Mount.' I imagine it was. And it is a pain which we in our turn must prepare ourselves to endure for the sake of the kingdom. It means we have to keep on deepening our understanding of the Gospel message and it requires each of us throughout our ministry to remain committed to continuing our formation, so that the account we give of the hope that is in us may not fall on deaf ears, but may be welcomed gladly. In particular, it can guide and encourage us as servants of the word.

7. See Donald Nicholl, *The Beatitude of Truth: Reflections of a Lifetime* (London, 1997), pp. 5–6.

9

Servants of the Word

(i)

WHEN the Second Vatican Council described preaching as 'the first task of priests', it was not thinking of something confined to the pulpit; it meant conversation and teaching and reflection on contemporary problems as well (see *Presbyterorum Ordinis*, n. 4). The service of the word, therefore, is more than a duty to be done. If we are going to make the word real for others, it must first be real for us. It is meant to flow from who we are. Once again, all who have been baptized must bear witness to the gospel – we notice the familiar refrain – but once again, too, those who have been ordained have a particular responsibility laid on them to be servants of the word. How can we prepare ourselves? It is a personal question.

In 107 Ignatius of Antioch was taken in chains to be executed in Rome. On his journey he wrote seven letters. In one of them, addressed to the Ephesians, he observed, 'A man who has mastered the utterances of Jesus will also be able to understand his silence, and thus reach full spiritual maturity' (Ignatius, *Ephesians* 15). It is a remark which makes me catch my breath. I am drawn by the idea that those who grasp what Jesus taught, are led beyond that into the silence, the mystery, from which it came, and so come to maturity. To be servants of the word, we must know the teaching. Learning, study, is important, because, as we have just seen, we must be able to account for the hope that is in us. But we must also know more than the teaching; we must be familiar with the silence. And so our preaching can be the fruit of spiritual maturity. If we are going to make the word real for others, it must first be real for us.

Earlier I suggested that prayer is like a foreign language, something which is unfamiliar at first, but which can become natural.[1] When it does so, it changes our culture, the way we live. Our service of the word is similar. Prayer, study, and the wide range of our experience all have a part to play in forming us as preachers. It is not a question of preaching all the time in the pejorative sense. We must never become preachy. But we can become more alert to the presence of the Spirit in a way that feeds our service of the word. And if we want to understand better what that means, then it may help to remember what Paul once told the Corinthians. 'Now we have received', he explained to them, 'not the spirit of the world, but the Spirit which is from God, that we might understand the gifts bestowed on us by God. And we impart this in words not taught by human wisdom but taught by the Spirit, interpreting spiritual things to those who possess the Spirit' (1 Corinthians 2:12–13). He is describing a process.

He is talking first about receiving the Spirit which comes from God, not the spirit of the world; he is speaking of giftedness, not simply of achievement. And then he says that we receive the Spirit for a purpose: so that we might understand what we have received from God; it is not a matter of human wisdom alone, but of penetrating the divine mysteries. And finally he explains that this understanding is not something which we keep to ourselves, but we share it with others, interpreting spiritual things to those who possess the Spirit. It is not an easy passage, but it is instructive. When I have thought about it, I have puzzled over it and wanted to explain it to others, but for a while was unsure how to do so. Then one day I found I was helped by a rather unlikely analogy. I remembered a television programme I had seen about city foxes. These animals would only come out at night, under cover of darkness, and so they were hidden. They could not be observed. But they could be filmed and so watched even at night by using a special light, infra-red light,

1. See above, p. 92.

which was invisible to the unaided natural eye; it was, however, suited to the camera, it was light for the camera's eye. And it made me think how the deep truths of the gospel may be hidden from us, shrouded in darkness like a fox; but that the gifts of the Spirit enlighten the eyes of our minds, they supply a special light, like infra-red light assisting the camera's eye, so that we can see what otherwise would be hidden. And we go on to share what we have perceived with others. The Spirit's presence illuminates us.

Through prayer, study, and experience we become more sensitive to the Spirit. Our love for the Scriptures becomes more intimate. We find that we notice connections which we might otherwise have missed. That's one of the effects of intimacy. People in love see connections that others don't. Those who are ordained accept quite specifically the responsibility to be servants of the word. We serve it in particular by being alert to connections. We all have stories to tell. Let me tell one of mine, about Simon Roberts. His parents have kindly allowed me to do so.

It is always difficult to preach when someone has committed suicide. Simon was schizophrenic. He was in his twenties and had struggled with his illness for thirteen years. He had done well. He had great generosity. If he had two cigarettes, he'd give one away. He was interested in others and untouched by envy. He loved poetry and philosophy. He had a sense of humour and a sense of adventure. He dreamed dreams. Besides that, in practical terms, he had his own apartment and was well cared for by his family and friends and the social services, but he was becoming tired. He would sometimes refer to approaching the end. Then, when his parents once decided that they would take a short break, he took the opportunity to walk into the river and drown himself. They were devastated. How could they be comforted?

In the days between his death and the funeral, I had to go to a meeting in London. On the way back I used the train journey to read Vincent Nichols' book on the mass, *Promise of Future Glory*, which I had been sent for review. I noticed there something which had never occurred to me before, the literal meaning of the word 'diabolic'. I've just been re-reading the passage; it is hard to see now how it had the impact it had then, but in those days before the requiem, it struck me with force.[2] What is diabolic is literally what tears us apart. And I thought how Simon's schizophrenia had been diabolic, not as a form of demonic possession, but as something which had truly torn him apart. And I realized as well that 'symbolic' has the same root, but the opposite meaning. What is symbolic brings together what has been separate. And Simon, torn apart, had found healing, however tragically, by entering water, water which recalls baptism, death and resurrection.

At the same time, I was also reading Hilary Davies' sonnets on the Stations of the Cross. There are two references to water. One was too painful to use. The second sonnet, 'Jesus Receives his Cross', contains these lines:

> When, and how, we shall receive it
> We do not know; . . .
> For her, a son wading into the tide; . . .

But the final sonnet, 'Jesus is Laid in the Tomb', pictures Joseph of Arimathea scrambling to prepare for the crucified Jesus the tomb intended for himself and ends inside the tomb with the line,

> Down the underworld walls the water hishes, victory, victory.[3]

How the sound of that water moved me.

I did not, of course, use this material in my homily in the way that I'm describing it here, although I made reference to Simon's illness as something which had torn him apart, but which now had been healed. I am wanting rather to illustrate how, when the Scriptures absorb us and we are trying to be servants of the word, all sorts of points may touch us. We see

2. See Vincent Nichols, *Promise of Future Glory: Reflections on the Mass* (London, 1997), pp. 45–6.
3. Davies, *In a Valley of this Restless Mind* (London, 1997), pp. 18, 24.

connections which might otherwise have passed unnoticed. They can help us directly or indirectly to make the word available for those who need it.

(ii)

When we are preaching, that is what we are trying to do, to help make the word come alive. In our liturgy, we honour the Bible and the Lectionary, we carry the Book of the Gospels in procession and incense it; sometimes we bless the congregation with it. But after all what the books contain is print on pages. What is needed is for the words to be read, and particularly for them to be read out loud.

In the eucharistic liturgy, bread and wine are taken, words are spoken over them, and they are changed: what had been bread and wine has become the body and blood of Christ. Christ is really present. We are familiar with that, but we may fail to notice something similar in the liturgy of the word. We take the text and read it out. What had been print on a page is transformed, dead letters are changed, the word comes alive, the Word who is Christ. Here too, when the word is proclaimed, Christ is really present. And what happens next? Later in the mass, the sacred elements, hosts and the cup, are distributed; people, as we say, come to communion, they communicate. And it is the same in the liturgy of the word. The Christ who has become present through the reading of sacred Scripture, is to be communicated to the people. In the homily, the Word is to be broken open, and distributed, so that those present may receive him.

That, as we have noticed already, is 'the first task' of those who have been ordained. They are to preach the Gospel of God. Studies in homiletics have become common, especially since the Second Vatican Council. The document, *Fulfilled in your Hearing*, which was produced by the North American Bishops' Conference in 1982, is still a valuable text. But the question for those who have to preach remains, how? How are we to make the word come alive? Again, it is a personal question. When we recognize this task for what it is, we may feel overwhelmed. Some people are more at ease with words than others, but all the same confidence can be fragile. I gain encouragement from the comment of a child years ago about priests and preaching. She said, 'Some priests are very nervous and they don't know what to say, but they shouldn't be, because they are just like us.' People are understanding. All the same, we shouldn't presume on their good nature. There are some fairly straightforward, practical points, which it is worth bearing in mind.

(iii)

Firstly, those who have to preach, should try to make it interesting. That may be obvious, but is not always as easy as we might expect. The last two weeks of the liturgical year, devoted to apocalyptic texts, will, I suspect, challenge most people's ingenuity. But we should try to have something worth saying and to make it interesting. A helpful test may be to ask, would I want to listen to this myself? Of course, the criterion isn't foolproof. Some of the most boring people in the world, those entranced by the sound of their own voices, would wish for nothing else.

Secondly, take care to edit well. Don't try to say it all. It is not necessary. I like this remark by Newman: 'I lay it down as a fundamental Canon, that a Sermon to be effective must be imperfect.'[4] He was discussing this very point in answer to criticism that his first volume of sermons had not covered the whole range of doctrine. He was saying that it did not need to.

Thirdly, linked to efficient editing, is timing. How many good sermons are ruined because they are too long. When the point has been made, finish. Could something more be said? Yes. Is there a further aspect which could be explained? Of course, there

4. See Thomas Gornall SJ (ed.), *The Letters and Diaries of John Henry Newman* V (Oxford, 1981), p. 38.

is. But leave it for another occasion. Again, if you weren't doing the talking, would you want to go on listening?

Fourthly, allied to this last issue, there is a need for humility. Preachers should always be modest about how much difference they are making. Two stories can illustrate what I mean.

One is told against himself by an American friend of mine who is now happily in good health. On Maundy Thursday some years ago he preached what he told me was a marvellous homily. 'I know I say it who shouldn't,' he said, 'but it was terrific. I really gave it to them.' Afterwards, he went to wash the feet of parishioners and, while he was doing so, he had a massive heart attack. There was alarm in the church, an ambulance was summoned, sirens blared out, paramedics cared for him, and he was taken away to hospital down the aisle on a stretcher. When some kind of normality had been restored, the mass continued with one of the assistant priests who had been concelebrating, now presiding. After it, as the congregation left the church, one parishioner took his hand and shook it warmly. 'Father,' he said, 'that was a wonderful homily you gave.' Let's not suppose people are noticing the preacher too much.

The second story I heard by chance from Cardinal Leon-Joseph Suenens who was then Archbishop of Malines-Bruxelles. In February 1977 Suenens gave the University Mission in Oxford. I was due to return to work at the Catholic Chaplaincy later that year and Crispian Hollis, who was the chaplain there at that time, invited me to come as an assistant missioner, based at the Chaplaincy, as a way of familiarizing myself with the place again. I was happy to accept. During the mission, Suenens held a small press conference which I was able to attend. I remember that one journalist asked him what effect he was hoping the mission would have. The Cardinal said he didn't know. The journalist pressed him, saying he must have some aim or hope for the mission. Suenens said, 'No.' The man was incredulous. Then Suenens said, 'Let me tell you a story. There was once a famous preacher and one day, during one of his sermons, a man in the congregation underwent a conversion.

After the service, he went to speak to the preacher in the sacristy, to tell him what had happened. And the famous preacher, who was a little vain, as famous preachers tend to be, asked him, "I wonder if you can remember what it was that I said which made such an impression on you. It might be helpful on some future occasion." "Oh, yes," the man replied, "I remember clearly. It was that moment when you said, 'Here I finish the first part of my sermon and move to the second.' And I thought, Right, I must finish with the first part of my life and start another." ' There is plenty of scope for modesty when we preach. Who knows what may strike those who are listening?

Finally, good liturgy is like good theatre. It has tension, pace, momentum. If the priest is not only preaching, but for ever pausing to supply a commentary, indicating the way different themes are present, that quality will be destroyed. Imagine going to see a play in which from time to time members of the cast broke off to point out the significance of what was going on or read the stage directions as well as their parts. The impact would be lost. Priests have the opportunity to introduce the mass; there is the vital place which the homily enjoys; there is even the chance to comment before the final blessing. Extra interjections will be wearisome, irritating, and distracting. They are obstacles to prayer, leaving the congregation wondering with exasperation, 'When will it ever end?'

There are many more practical points to assist preachers, but these few are examples. They are less a matter of homiletics and more to do with the preacher: be interesting, edit wisely, watch the time, be humble, develop a sense of theatre. As servants of the word, we can do great good or cause much harm.

(iv)

This vocation may seem overwhelming, but we should not be discouraged. The word itself can revive us. In his commentary on the Diatesseron St Ephraem remarked, 'The thirsty man rejoices when he drinks and he is not downcast when he cannot empty the fountain . . . if your thirst is quenched and the fountain is not exhausted you can drink from it again whenever you are thirsty'.[5] He was likening the word of God to such a fountain; it does not run dry. Consider, for example, the parable of the sower going out to sow (see Mark 4:1–9, 13–20). It is very familiar and long and we may feel that it has nothing more to teach us, but like the fountain we may not have exhausted it yet. It seems to me to have something very special to say to those who are servants of the word. Cast the personae.

In the first place and perhaps most obviously, the preacher can be cast as the sower. Those who are servants of the word are called to scatter seed. We don't know where it may fall, what effect our words may have. Points, inconsequential to us, may touch people in ways we had never imagined. I don't suppose I am the only preacher who has been thanked effusively after mass for a remark which was actually a passing reference, added on the spur of the moment, which has nonetheless plainly meant much to that listener at least. We are sowers. We scatter seed, but cannot predict the result. We should, however, try to avoid rocky ground. Don't scatter it there deliberately. In other words, try not to be a bore: edit wisely, watch the time, be humble, and develop a sense of theatre.

Next, it helps to realize that we are also the ground. The seed is scattered in us. So what kind of ground am I? One approach to this parable makes it like an examination of conscience for those who are listening. What kind of ground are you? the preacher asks the congregation. Are you the pathway, rather than the field? Are you rocky ground, where the soil is thin? Are you that part of the field which is choked by brambles and briars? Or are you rich soil, capable of producing a fine harvest? When I put the question to myself, I find I have to answer that I am none of these alone. I am rather the whole landscape, partly pathway, partly thin soil, partly overgrown, and (I hope) there is

5. It is the patristic reading in the Office of Readings for the Sixth Sunday in Ordinary Time.

some rich fruitful soil in me as well. I suspect many of us would make the same reply. We are the earth which receives the seed. We are invited to cultivate it to make it yield a still richer harvest.

And finally, we are called to be the seed as well. That is not arrogance. I do not mean that preachers should preach about themselves, but that our lives should reflect what we are saying. It is Pope Paul VI's point again that witnesses are more welcome today than teachers and that, when teachers are welcome, it is because they are also witnesses (see *Evangelii Nuntiandi*, n. 41). It is not a matter simply of what we do, but who we are. Our lives must become living gospel. Those who preach must constantly be building up their familiarity with sacred Scripture. We open our minds and hearts, so that the seed which is Christ may take root in us and shape us. We become the seed. It will not be easy. The risk of discipleship is never far away. Once again, we are reminded that we are being invited to echo St Paul, crucified with Christ, so that we ourselves live no longer, but Christ lives in us. Then what we communicate can truly be that Christ present within us.

Servants of the word are sower, soil, and seed. We are called to proclaim the good news. And we know that it doesn't end there. What we proclaim we must also celebrate.

10

Celebrating Mysteries

(i)

For some Christians worship is conceived ideally as something spontaneous. Patterns in services may recur in fact, but there is meant to be an openness to the Spirit which allows for freedom in liturgy. In these circumstances, the sermon is often prized highly. It will be the jewel in the crown. A poor preacher, or even a good preacher on a poor day, may sense the pressure. If the sermon falls flat, if its message doesn't inspire, the congregation may feel let down. Those words most of all were what they had come for. By contrast, in a Catholic setting, vital as the homily is, the value of the liturgy will not be determined by it. What is proclaimed in word must also be celebrated in action. Those who are ordained are called to be servants of the word, as we have seen; it is their first task. But, if their words are weak, all is not lost; they are called to celebrate mysteries, the sacraments, as well. When they baptize, they bring people to birth in the people of God; when they absolve sins, they reconcile them to God and to the Church; when they anoint the sick, they relieve those who are ill; and when they celebrate mass, they offer Christ's sacrifice sacramentally (see *Presbyterorum Ordinis*, n. 5). These actions do not depend on the quality of the minister's performance or holiness for their validity. When those who are ordained celebrate them as the Church wishes them to be celebrated, then they are Christ's instruments, he acts in them, and their acts are efficacious. There is a plainly objective aspect to these celebrations.

To know that effective celebration does not depend on me is a relief, but it must not become an excuse. The Second Vatican

Council pulled no punches. The Constitution on the Sacred Liturgy declared: 'Pastors of souls must, therefore, realize that, when liturgy is celebrated, something more is required than the laws governing valid and lawful celebration. It is their duty also to ensure that the faithful take part fully aware of what they are doing, actively engaged in the rite and enriched by it', lest they receive its grace in vain (*Sacrosanctum Concilium*, n. 11). Ministers can hinder the mysteries they celebrate. There is a delicate balance here. It is not good enough for celebrants to become involved so personally that the congregation almost seems to be ignored, but neither will it be sufficient for them to become so absorbed by their relationship with the congregation that they freewheel through the liturgy. It sounds obvious, but the balance is not caught easily. Before we go any further, it may help to pause and consider what is being asked of us. Liturgical prayer is prayer of a special kind.

(ii)

Good liturgy requires personal involvement. That should go without saying. The detached celebrant will be detected at once. But some degree of detachment is also necessary, a sensitivity to the way the liturgy is being presented. How can these two elements be combined? We have seen already that a homilist is helped by realizing what makes good theatre, pace, tension, momentum. If liturgy has something in common with drama, and it does, then acting skills may have something to teach us here as well.

One description of acting expresses precisely what I have in mind. On stage, two aspects need to be held together. The actor, David Burke, has called acting a 'twin-track mental activity'. He explains:

> In one track runs the role, demanding thoughts ranging from, say, gentle amusement to towering rage. Then there is the second track that is monitoring the performance:

> executing the right moves, body language, and voice level; taking note of audience reaction and keeping an eye on fellow actors; coping with emergencies such as a missing prop or a faulty lighting cue. These two tracks run parallel, night by night. If one should go wrong, then it is likely that the other will misbehave, too.[1]

What a splendid analogy for good liturgy, except that priests are not acting. Liturgical prayer requires a twin-track mental activity as well. On the one hand, priests need to be absorbed in what they are doing, caught up prayerfully in the celebration, their role, while, on the other, they too need to be aware of their body language and audibility, what is taking place around them in the sanctuary and what is happening in the body of the church, the responsiveness of the congregation; they also need to be conscious of missing 'props', the non-appearance, perhaps, of gifts at the offertory, or a missed music cue from the organ loft. Good liturgy needs both: genuine prayerfulness and sensitivity to surroundings. Lose either and the liturgy will flop. That must not be allowed to happen. In the liturgy our highest responsibilities are expressed.

When those who are ordained celebrate the sacraments, and most of all when they celebrate the eucharist which is 'the source and summit of all preaching of the Gospel' (*Presbyterorum Ordinis*, n. 5), they act in the person of Christ and offer sacrifice to God in the name of all the people (see *Lumen Gentium*, nn. 10, 28). So it is 'in the eucharistic assembly that they exercise in a supreme degree their sacred functions', gathering the people, proclaiming the Gospel, and making present until he comes again the unique sacrifice of Christ, 'offering himself once for all a spotless victim to the Father' (see *Lumen Gentium*, n. 28). Ministerial priesthood is realized here.

It is time to consider at a deeper level what it means to

1. See Michael Frayn and David Burke, *Celia's Secret: an Investigation* (London, 2000), p. 21.

celebrate mysteries and in particular to reflect on what it means to celebrate the eucharist.

(iii)

We are told that on the night before he died Jesus was at supper with his disciples. According to our tradition, they were celebrating Passover. During the meal he took bread and gave thanks and broke it and handed it to them – it was part of the ritual – but he also did something else: he identified himself with that broken bread, saying, 'This is my body which is broken for you'. And then in the same way he took the cup and gave it to them and said to them, 'This cup which is poured out for you is the new covenant in my blood.' We can only wonder what the disciples made of these words at the time.

Shortly afterwards they went out and made their way to the Mount of Olives. A little later Judas arrived with guards to arrest Jesus and his companions deserted him. We are familiar with what happened next. He was interrogated and tortured, scourged, mocked, and crowned with thorns. Finally, he was condemned to be crucified, was led away, and was put to death. He died surprisingly quickly and was taken down and buried before sunset and the beginning of the Sabbath.

The disciples came together in fear, but Mary Magdalene, accompanied perhaps by some other women, went to the tomb early in the morning after the Sabbath, hoping that she could find someone to help her roll back the stone, so that she might anoint the body. She arrived, however, to find the stone rolled away already and the tomb empty. She was bewildered. But then Jesus appeared to her. Later he appeared to others, to Simon Peter, to two disciples on the road to Emmaus, to those who were gathered in the upper room, and to a group of disciples at the lakeside in Galilee. Others saw him as well and they came to believe that the one who was their master and friend and who had been crucified and had died, had been raised from the dead. Here was a Passover of another order. The Lamb had been slain, the body broken, and blood shed. The passion, death, and resurrection of Jesus were not merely episodes in his life of which we might well be in awe; they proclaim as victorious the Father's love for us, revealed by Jesus, a love which seeks our reconciliation. By dying he had destroyed death and by rising he had restored life. The disciples came to see the events of the evening of his arrest in a new light. And they remembered that Jesus had told them to do again what he had done, to break bread and to share the cup in remembrance of him. And so they did.

Within thirty years at the most we find St Paul writing to the Corinthians about these matters, not as a novelty, not simply as a way of interpreting an extraordinary evening, but as something established: 'I received from the Lord what I also delivered to you' (1 Corinthians 11:23–6). From the earliest times the followers of Jesus have gathered for the breaking of bread, for the celebration of eucharist.

We see three moments intertwined inextricably: the supper, the cross, and the mass. The supper in the upper room anticipated the death on the cross, while the eucharist, which recalls the supper, carries us back to Calvary: at every mass we stand at the foot of the cross. No mass repeats Christ's sacrifice. Each mass brings us into its presence. Jesus' love led him to the cross and so the Father raised him up. Our acceptance of that love gathers us at the cross and brings us reconciliation.

How is that possible? It is difficult to describe the process, but it may help to remember in these circumstances how we should understand memory, time, and word. For us memory is most often just passive, nostalgic, a gazing back to times which have passed, but it does not need to be like that. Sometimes memories, memorials, are active, they enable us to make the past present. For the Jews memorials are like that, and Jesus said, 'Do this in memory of me'. Then we tend to assume that time is just quantitative, a measurement, and we forget that it can also be a name for a kind of time, Christmastime, springtime, holiday time. There was a time for redemption. And we tend to presume that words are just static, descriptive, relating what has been. Again, they do not need to be. Words can be powerful, for example when someone declares their love. To be told, 'I love you', can overwhelm us. And God's words are dynamic. They effect what they proclaim: 'God said, "Let there be light"; and there was light'; and Jesus said, 'This is my body, this is my blood.'

To recall what I have said elsewhere,

> When we recognize that memory can be active as well as passive, that time can possess a quality, not merely supply a measurement, and that words can make real what they proclaim, and when we realize that every mass is such an active memorial in a particular time, using words filled with power, we can come to see how each mass is not a repetition of Calvary, but gathers us on every occasion at the foot of the cross. We are always there.[2]

The eucharist above all is the mystery which those who are ordained are called to celebrate. They gather people together, proclaim the gospel, and make Christ really present in the sacred elements. Someone in formation may sometimes say, 'If I could just celebrate one mass, I would die happy.' It is a natural thought when we reflect on the awesome character of the responsibility laid on us, the wonder of what we are required to do. They may also, however, be reflecting that understanding of priesthood when the emphasis was placed distinctly, almost exclusively, on the celebration of the eucharist, on cultic power. Priests, it was said, were those who effected daily the miracle of the mass. That was the viewpoint, as we have noticed, which held sway from the Middle Ages until the Second Vatican Council.[3] But this whole question of cult is highly complex. Jesus was not a priest. He was a layman. Only the Epistle to the Hebrews describes

2. Strange, *Living Catholicism* (London, 2001), pp. 97–8; quotation at p. 98.
3. See above, pp. 41–2.

him as a priest. Has that one document misled us? Or perhaps it is teaching us something more profound. In November 1987 Timothy Radcliffe, who has since been Master of the Dominicans, wrote an article for *New Blackfriars* called 'Christ in Hebrews: Cultic Irony'.[4] There he dealt directly with this issue, the way the understanding of cult, of worship, was transformed in Christ. Some key points are most instructive for our purpose.

(iv)

In the first place, it is noteworthy that cultic language was the traditional way of speaking about God's relationship with creation and creation at first is a matter of distinction, of separation: most fundamentally, something comes out of nothing. And so the language of the liturgy also spoke about distinctiveness, about separation, of order from chaos, of light from darkness, of day from night, of the waters above from the waters below. It also supplied the basis for social distinctions: of Jew from Gentile, of male from female, of priestly from lay. And integral to these distinctions was the concept of ritual purity: the clean must be kept separate from the unclean. This, putting it very simply, is the essential backcloth to the Letter to the Hebrews: the Old Testament priest was such by virtue of his separation from others. He was able to purify because he was himself free from all impurity. He was uncontaminated, a man apart. But, Radcliffe observes, 'the author of Hebrews turns this principle on its head and bases the priesthood of Christ on his solidarity, closeness, to others'.

Secondly, what underpins this new theology of solidarity is something more fundamental still, a transformation of God's relationship to suffering and death: 'God had been perceived as the source of all life and holiness precisely in his separation from death. The purity regulations aim at creating the maximum

4. Timothy Radcliffe, 'Christ in Hebrews: Cultic Irony', *New Blackfriars* (November 1987), pp. 494–504.

distance between the corpse and the Holy of Holies. The corpse was the ultimately impure object . . . It radiates impurity as God radiates holiness'. It is not difficult to understand why, in the parable of the Good Samaritan, the priest and the Levite should have walked by on the other side; they gave the man who had been attacked by robbers and left as half-dead a wide berth; they had no wish to be contaminated, to become unclean. 'But in Christ', Radcliffe continues, 'God's creative act happened in a grasping of the ultimate impurity and its transformation so that "through death he might destroy him who has the power of death" ' (p. 499).

God now is the creator who raises the dead. Everything is changed. Christ is perfected, but by suffering; 'he is ordained by immersion in the impure' (p. 500). He is the great High Priest, but he does not save us, heal us, cleanse us, by remaining apart. He comes out of love to share our wounded state, but without being conformed to it; and so he transforms it. He cleanses us by immersing himself in our sinful condition. He embraces wounded humanity. His new priesthood is not lofty or exclusive. On the contrary, solidarity and inclusiveness have become essential. Then by our baptism we walk with him in newness of life and so become a part of his priesthood.

When I think about this solidarity, I think of Gerald Murray. I buried him in 1999. I had known him for twenty-five years, but for the last twenty-three, following a heart attack and a stroke, he had been crippled and had not spoken. He accepted and endured his condition in a way which could only inspire respect and admiration. His grandson, Timothy, paid him tribute at the end of the requiem mass. Now in his late twenties, Tim has himself been severely handicapped physically from his birth. He told us that his grandfather in his silence 'has taught me more about myself and about the power of the human spirit than could have possibly been expressed through words'. Gerald's disability had helped him see how he could cope with his own. And he added that he knew that his mother and his uncles and aunts had wanted him and his cousins to know their grandfather as they had known him. 'Well,' he said, 'we did. But we knew him at a stage in his life when he had something different to learn about himself and something new to teach us.' It seems to me a golden remark and one which casts light too on the way Christ's suffering redeems ours. When we follow his footsteps, we have to carry burdens. Suffering is never easy and sometimes special people, like Gerald, are called to bear it in unforeseen and unimaginable ways. Most of us have to do that somehow. We too find ourselves 'immersed in the impure'. However, when we remain faithful in spite of suffering, then we support others and help lighten their loads. That is the essence of the tribute that Gerald's grandson was paying him. In his suffering and by his endurance he was exercising a Christlike priesthood. It is a gift for all the baptized. In the Preface at the Chrism Mass in Holy Week, it is expressed in these words, 'Christ gives the dignity of a royal priesthood to the people he has made his own.'

Then we are told that some others are chosen by the laying on of hands. Christ 'calls them to lead [the Father's] holy people in love, nourish them by [his] word, and strengthen them through the sacraments'. Here once more the vital tasks of ministerial priesthood are named: those who are ordained are to serve in love, preach the gospel, and celebrate the mysteries. And then we are also told: 'Father, they are to give their lives in your service and for the salvation of your people as they strive to grow in the likeness of Christ and honour him by their courageous witness of faith and love.' They must be prepared for sacrifice.

(v)

For many of those who are ordained, celebrating the mysteries and most especially celebrating the eucharist is their prize and consolation. It is a privilege beyond compare. They speak the words of consecration. As Pope John Paul has said, they put their voices 'at the disposal of the One who spoke these words in the Upper Room and who desires that they should be repeated in every generation by all those who in the Church ministerially share in his priesthood' (*Ecclesia de Eucharistia*, n. 5). This privilege must never be underestimated. In his Encyclical, *Ecclesia de Eucharistia*, the Pope recalls some of the places in which he has said mass. Every priest can do the same. I think, first, of the masses I have said daily in the parishes, colleges, and chaplaincies in which I have been called to serve since my ordination in 1969; I think of masses I have celebrated in Israel, on the Mount of Olives, in the wilderness between Jerusalem and Jericho, and by the lakeside in Galilee; and I recall as well, especially in these more recent years occasions when, as rector of a seminary preparing men for ministerial priesthood in many parts of the world, I have been able to travel to ordinations and have celebrated mass in other, for me less predictable, places, in Tripoli, in an open field in Kenya, and at the conclusion of a Eucharistic Congress in Moscow in 2000, after which more than a thousand people processed through the streets with the Blessed Sacrament, assisted courteously by the Russian police and watched respectfully by the local people. It would have astonished Josef Stalin.

The privilege of celebrating mass, however, is not to be grasped as a mark of distinctive, superior status, designed to set priests apart. There was indeed that long period when priests were seen as cultic figures. However, in his article on Christ in Hebrews, Timothy Radcliffe noticed an instructive coincidence. He pointed out that the typical New Testament word for 'community' was *koinonia* and that the connotation for words derived from it tended to be negative. *Koinos* means 'common' and by Jesus' time had come to mean 'impure' (p. 501). Our own usage can still reflect that. When we call something common, we are often referring to something we hold dear, such as our common values or the common good. At the same time, when we say, for example, that a person's clothes are common, we mean they look cheap and nasty. And since 1987, the coincidence has moved on further. All the major church documents from about that time, especially those on the lay faithful (*Christifideles Laici*), on priestly formation (*Pastores Dabo Vobis*), and on Religious Life (*Vita Consecrata*), have turned to *koinonia* as supplying their principal way of speaking about the Church. The Church as communion has been recognized as the central and fundamental idea of the ecclesiology employed by the Second Vatican Council.

Within this Church Christ has transformed what it means to be a priest. As we have seen, he has turned it upside down. The priests of the New Testament are not like other priests. And those chosen by the laying on of hands are not separated from the people, but are consecrated for their service. The risk of discipleship is never far away. To be ordained is not a summons to grandeur, but an invitation to live with the tension between the precious and the impure. Besides proclaiming the word and celebrating mysteries the ordained are called to be leaders as well. This community which is holy, is also in need of renewal, because its common life which is precious and which we cherish, is sometimes common in that other sense, cheap and nasty, sinful and in need of redemption. Its leaders cannot hold themselves aloof. They must be 'immersed in the impure'.

11

Servant and Leader

(i)

THOSE who are ordained are called to be leaders of the community. It is the third major task laid upon them. They must proclaim the word and celebrate sacraments, but they must give leadership as well. This third task is perhaps the most problematical, because they must lead like the Son of man who came not to be served, but to serve. And there we find the problem. Leadership and service are not natural partners. Timothy Radcliffe has put it as succinctly as anyone: 'The idea of the priest as servant and leader is beautiful, but the words tend to pull in opposite directions. Servants are not usually supposed to lead, like bossy butlers.'[1] And in fact the Council Decree on the presbyterate endorsed this tension: priests are set apart by virtue of their ordination, but they must not be separated from the people; they must bear witness to a life not of this earth, but their service will be powerless if they remain aloof from this earthly life and its circumstances; they must not be conformed to this world, but they should live in it as good shepherds, who know their sheep and lead others to hear the voice of Christ (see *Presbyterorum Ordinis*, n. 3). This tension will not be easy to handle. This is leadership immersed in the impure. How is it to be exercised?

The point is not new. Pope Gregory the Great wrestled with this very issue and we read his thoughts each year in the breviary

1. Timothy Radcliffe, 'That your joy may be full', Address to the National Conference of Priests of England and Wales, September 2002, p. 2.

on 3 September, his feast. Gregory declared that as Pope he had to live on the heights in order to give help to those in his care. But he knew it made no sense for him to hold himself aloof. And so he wrote: 'If I preserved the rigorously inflexible mode of utterance that my conscience dictates, I know that the weaker sort of men would recoil from me and that I could never attract them to the goal I desire for them. So I must frequently listen patiently to their aimless chatter.' Here is a man who is aware of his high responsibilities, but who is prepared not to stand apart. And he recognized his own vulnerability as well. He continued: 'Because I am weak myself I am drawn gradually into idle talk and I find myself saying the kind of thing that I didn't even care to listen to before. I enjoy lying back where I once was loath to stumble.' Gregory was a leader, but he was also immersed in the community. He was aware of its impurity and his own weakness.

This idea, immersion in the impure, is not used as a judgement to condemn the community, but rather because it reflects, as we have noticed, the understanding of priesthood unveiled in the New Testament and in so doing corresponds to a theme which has run through these pages like a thread: the identity of those who are ordained is to be discovered within the community, not by separation from it. Leaders too are not simply set apart. They are caught up in the complexity. There is a fine dovetailing. It may help to draw the picture together.

We have seen that what people should expect to find in those of us who have been ordained is not their exclusive preserve. So Jesus is master, friend, and indeed brother to all the baptized; none of his followers is immune from the risk of discipleship; all Christians are called to human maturity, honest loving, and lives of prayer, and to give an account of their hope; and it is not only ministerial priests who proclaim the word, celebrate sacraments, and offer leadership, because even these particular tasks are not performed in isolation. Those who can find essential difference only by separation will be disturbed by this situation; they may feel threatened; but the Scriptures constantly urge us, 'Do not be afraid.' The identity of those who have been ordained is not to be restricted to those actions and powers which they alone possess, but must rather be recognized in the way they fulfil their calling. They follow the path followed by all Christians, but in a way that is particular to them. What way is that? In a striking expression used by R. Scott Appleby, speaking to the National Federation of Priests' Councils of the United States in June 2003, to be ordained is to be 'a sign for the average Christian; . . . an intensified embodiment of the priesthood of all the faithful'.[2] And to be that sign or embodiment begins to show us immediately what is meant by offering leadership as a service. It is the point we have recognized before: what is a blessing found in the baptized is expected of the ordained. The earlier question returns: how is this leadership to be exercised?

(ii)

It will be useful, first of all, to put the question into historical perspective and Scott Appleby's overview is a valuable aid.[3] Although he is not examining leadership directly, but the various models of priesthood which have emerged since 1930, it is the issue which is constantly implicit in what he is describing. And he is, of course, speaking about the Church in America, but, as developments there tend to take place before they happen elsewhere, his remarks have particular clarity and are all the more instructive.

Appleby identifies three models. The first he calls the all-purpose priest, who was a kind of general practitioner. He did everything. He did not empower others to act within the parish, nor even on its behalf in the world. He alone represented the parish. One crisp sentence captures the type by getting inside his mind: 'It did not occur to him that significant apostolic service might occur apart from his sacerdotal office' (p. 53).

2. R. Scott Appleby, 'Historical Overview: Priests in America, 1930–2002', *Origins*, vol. 33, no. 4 (5 June 2003), p. 64. He was quoting Joseph Byrne, writing in 1988.
3. See *ibid.*, pp. 50–64.

Appleby's survey begins from 1930, but this model had been operating for a long time before that. A second model began to emerge from the time of the Second Vatican Council in 1962. It can be seen as a reaction to the all-purpose priest. The general practitioner gave way to the specialist. The type took various forms: he may have been inspired by the demands of social justice and committed himself to the preferential option for the poor; he may have become what Appleby describes as the hyphenated priest, the priest-sociologist, the priest-psychiatrist, the priest-journalist, he was a specialist, an expert in some other field besides being a priest; then there were those who came to regard priesthood as itself a unique profession worthy of study; and there were those who began to form networks, whether as Priests' Councils or smaller support groups like Ministry to Priests and Jesus-Caritas. Whatever the form, and the forms plainly differed greatly, but could also overlap, the model was drawn to expertise, to some kind of specialization. And the third model which emerged from the mid-seventies on, is called by Appleby the orchestra leader, someone who integrates and supervises the individual skills and talents which others possess so as to establish a community with a common purpose.

Reading this overview I recognize similarities with the presentation of styles of leadership in *The Parish Project*, although with different emphases. This project was work commissioned in England some years ago by the Diocese of Portsmouth to help with parish renewal. It named neatly five different ways of leading as telling, selling, testing, resting, and joining. Those who tell are authoritarian and autocratic; they may get things done, but at a great price: the parishioners remain infantile. The sellers are much the same, but with a dash of charm added; however, people will soon recognize that they are being manipulated and feel used. Testers consult and make decisions only after widespread listening, but the decision is always theirs, they always get their own way; people come to feel discouraged, deprived of responsibility. Those at rest are at the other extreme altogether: under cover of delegating, they abdicate responsibility and create frustration and disillusionment. And the joiners work with people to discover the best way forward. This style is described as visionary and encouraging for all members of the parish, but it needs a lot of time, requires high skills, and assumes that those involved are mature enough to take responsibility for what they are doing and place the good of the parish above their own personal agendas.[4] Here leadership is seen to be service.

I find it instructive to set these two schemes, Appleby's and *The Parish Project's*, side by side. Then we may say that the tellers are unreconstructed all-purpose priests, while the sellers and testers are all-purpose as well, but reconstruction has begun. The resters probably see themselves as joiners, but sadly they are self-deluded; they offer nothing and so contribute nothing; it is noteworthy that they don't appear at all in Appleby's overview. And the joiners are Appleby's specialists on the way to becoming orchestra leaders. I am not trying to force equivalence, but the two accounts have much in common. In particular it is interesting to notice the way the broad band of specialists are in fact joiners. All of them were looking for ways to exercise their ministry better, to be involved more deeply. The very diversity of the model, seen from the viewpoint of its implications for leadership, is showing us how varied leadership may be, while their struggles should leave us with no illusions about the hazards to be faced. In these circumstances, we discover that leadership is a messy business. To lead in this way could be described aptly as immersion in the impure. It may be helpful to look at those struggles more closely.

(iii)

As we have seen, Appleby describes the specialists in four ways, those inspired by a concern for social justice, those with another

4. See John O'Shea, Declan Lang, Vicky Cosstick, Damian Lundy, *The Parish Project* (London, 1992), p. 89. This material on leadership is adapted from Thomas Sweetser and Carol Wisniewski Holden, *Leadership in a Successful Parish* (New York, 1987), pp. 15–20.

profession besides priesthood, those who emphasized priesthood itself as a profession, and those who became involved in the network of various kinds of priests' groups. All of them were joiners, but none of them found it easy.

Those who were inspired by social issues saw the priest as 'Christ walking the secular city, healing the wounds of injustice, liberating the oppressed'. But the high ideal was not fulfilled easily. Appleby explains, 'What seemed missing at times, however, was an effective and well-developed pastoral strategy based on a sophisticated appreciation of the needs of inner city parishes' (pp. 57–8). This way of life as a priestly ministry began to sag. The commitment, the ecumenical contacts, and the radical protest were significant and impressive and their value must not be ignored, but the lack of foundation, of that grounding in well-considered pastoral strategy, could make them divisive. Those parishioners who did not share their priest's particular enthusiasm could sometimes find they were dismissed as inadequate.

Those who acquired another profession besides their priesthood, the so-called 'hyphenated priest', displayed leadership by virtue of the very expertise which they had acquired. 'Advocates of the hyphenated priesthood', Appleby writes, 'welcomed the new professionalization and specialization as the perfect tonic for an ailing priesthood'. Why? Because, he goes on, 'it offered a new way of being present to the people of God' (p. 60). They were plainly joiners. They saw their style of ministry as an opportunity to be freed from many of the inhibitions which the institution had previously imposed on them, ideological inhibitions and those which were a part of the organization. They wanted to 'shape a new, more pluralistic and flexible church' (p. 60). The words are part of a quotation from Andrew Greeley, who is perhaps the archetypical hyphenated priest. Here too, however, there were difficulties. In particular, the other profession could become absorbing and so make priesthood seem irrelevant. Without a reasonably regular base in some specifically presbyteral work, like saying mass, hearing confessions, and preaching, it was difficult for the priestly dimension to remain secure.

It may seem to some that what both these first two groups needed was to get back to priestly work in the more narrowly defined sense and all would be well, but the solution is not so easy. After all, what was inspiring them, whether the demands of social justice or the opportunities for the apostolate which further specialization offered, was well perceived. They were responding to a genuine need. The tension came from the struggle to locate the proper place for more specific priestly work in what they were now doing. It was not a question of returning to that work alone, but ensuring that it could continue to play its proper regular part.

The third group may perhaps be seen almost in contrast with the second. They looked to the priesthood specifically. For them the priesthood to which they had been called was itself their profession. They developed a heightened awareness of its professional character. So it became an object of scientific study. What that study revealed, however, could be discouraging. 'These priests found themselves in a kind of limbo between two worlds', Appleby observes. 'They had not yet absorbed or personally appropriated the new insights and techniques of postconciliar priesthood, but they were aware that the ombudsman model was no longer sufficient to their needs or to the needs of their parishioners' (p. 61). They too were looking for a way to exercise their ministry more faithfully, but discovered they were out of step with a society become affluent. Many in fact coped well, but the strain told on others. Morale dipped. Some, instead of being signs of contradiction, reflected society's ways, adopting a kind of cafeteria approach to doctrine and discipline, doing what they pleased (pp. 61–2).

The fourth group in turn may seem to supply the necessary antidote for the third. They formed priests' associations, whether the more formal bodies like diocesan councils and senates or smaller support groups like Jesus-Caritas, Ministry for Priests, and the Emmaus Program. In their different ways they sought to give priests the support they needed, to help them be joiners. A renewed relationship between priests was the starting point, identified by Appleby, as necessary for them in addressing their role in the Church as an institution and in the parishes. Once again, however, it was not straightforward. Priests' senates were always consultative, never executive. The lack of power to make decisions and achieve goals bred frustration and led to confrontation. The National Federation of Priests' Councils was 'formed in 1968 as an independent association dedicated in part to coordinating and representing priests' concerns on a national level – another way of "ministering to the minister" ' (p. 62).

These models of priesthood all faced problems. To be a part of the communion, to become 'immersed in the impure', is never going to be free from difficulties. The collaborative kind of ministry which corresponds to that immersion is testing and costly. Whatever the differences between these models of priesthood, the priests who adopted them had one thing in common, they wanted to live out a renewed vision of priesthood more faithfully by being bound more deeply to the people with whom they worked. To put it simply, they wanted to be better servants. And Appleby concludes that each of these developments 'contributed significantly to the transformation of the priesthood and especially to the emergence of a way of priestly presence to the parish in the 1970s and 1980s which kept [the priest] in the parish' (p. 64). He calls that new style of presence 'the orchestra leader'. The very title is revealing. The deeper, more faithful vision, rooted in service, highlights a way of leading. According to Appleby, 'the orchestra leader perceived each parishioner as uniquely "called and gifted" for service to the church and to the world. As a representative of the universal church, his role is, in the words of the council, to elevate, purify and bring into closer conformity with Christ the fruits of lay ministry' (p. 64). Those who are ordained must lead the faithful to 'the full development' of their vocation (see *Presbyterorum Ordinis*, n. 6).

The joiners who seek to orchestrate others' gifts, are servants and their leadership is integral to that service, but we must probe the relationship between leadership and service more closely.

(iv)

Leadership and service seem at first to make unlikely partners. It is the point we noticed at the beginning. One common idea of a leader is someone with vision and the personality to influence others so as to make the vision real. There will be times when the priest must clearly be in charge and have the courage to take the decisions which are needed, welcome or unwelcome, popular or unpopular. There will be other times, however, when the leadership called for will be different. It will involve instead 'influencing the community to face its problems'.[5] And its particular problem may not be a problem as such, but rather its need to become the community it is meant to be, to achieve the full development of its vocation. Ronald A. Heifetz from the John F. Kennedy School of Leadership at Harvard University, whose phrase I have just quoted, has studied this very issue. He is less concerned with the dominant figure. His interest concentrates particularly on the way leadership is exercised so that both leader and people are involved. And that is precisely the kind of leadership which a priest needs to exercise most often. But how is it to be done?

(v)

It is important first of all to identify the nature of the problem. That is fundamental. People come to their leaders with problems, but not all problems are of the same kind. Heifetz makes a distinction between practical questions to which someone in authority should be able to give the answer, and issues which

5. See Ronald A. Heifetz, *Leadership Without Easy Answers* (Cambridge Massachusetts, 1994), p. 14. I have drawn heavily on this work in this section and readily acknowledge my debt.

can't be dealt with so simply because they require people to change. The former he calls technical problems, the latter adaptive challenges. The distinction is invaluable. When faced with a problem, leaders need to ask themselves what kind of problem it is, technical or adaptive. If they make a mistake, the consequences can be disastrous: they will be dithering over questions they should tackle and avoiding challenges by imposing solutions which fail to answer the need. As leaders, we have to be able to recognize the kind of question we are being asked and be decisive when decisiveness is appropriate; we must not shirk our responsibilities. But we also need to know how to handle the challenges which arise. It is those challenges which will normally provide the severest test. Heifetz proposes a strategy which has four elements.

Firstly, the challenge must be identified. Let me suggest a plausible scenario. You are a priest in a parish which is going to be combined with two others. You will still have responsibility for these people whose priest you have been for the past five years, but the new arrangement makes it more sensible for you to live in a different presbytery which is more central to the area. The adaptive challenges are many and obvious. First, how are these three parishes going to be woven into a single community? Then, how are gifts of the previously separate parishes going to be preserved? How is the parish where you used to live going to feel about you living elsewhere? Do they feel deprived? Have they lost 'their' priest? However, are the members of the other parishes, even the one where you are now living, going to feel that your heart is still really where you used to be? The questions could go on and on. First, identify the challenge.

Secondly, those questions are evidence of stress and distress. The situation is stressful and people will be distressed by it. Old, familiar, well-loved ways of living their Catholicism are being altered. Change is hard. The second element which Heifetz proposes, is the regulating of this distress. A lot of reassurance will be needed. People have to be helped to realize that change is not simply loss. Everything is not being taken from them. Difference need not mean deprivation. The new situation will bring blessings and benefits. The managing of this distress will take a lot of time. Timing may well be a key factor. Time may not always be available; perhaps a church has to be demolished sooner rather than later. Even so, it will be vital to regulate distress.

Thirdly, it is essential not to lose sight of the key issues. Heifetz speaks of directing disciplined attention to the issues. It will be a feature in caring for the distress. But that care must not cloud the purpose and reason for what is being done. These new plans are, of course, being put in place because there are fewer priests than there were, but reference to a shortage of priests is not helpful. I was referring to it once myself, and an older, wiser priest friend pulled me up short. 'Oh, really,' he said. 'So how many ought there to be? Do you think the Lord has established an ideal number?' Fewer priests may have been the immediate cause for such change, but we have to look for ways of being the Church in this new situation, ways in which our faith and commitment can be deepened and strengthened and the Church's mission realized more perfectly. 'The harvest is plentiful, but the labourers are few,' Jesus told his disciples. 'Pray therefore the Lord of the harvest to send out labourers into his harvest' (Matthew 9:37–8). If we apply that to ministerial priesthood alone, those who live in the prosperous Western world may feel saddened today; but apply it to ministry more generally and we may be filled with wonder at the way that prayer has been answered through the abundance of catechists and lay ministries. I will never forget a Saturday in the mid-nineties in the Shrewsbury Diocese when we held a special day for parish catechists. If my memory is correct, at least two hundred and fifty people were there. Addressing the group, Bishop Brian Noble reminded everyone that such a gathering would have been unthinkable thirty years earlier. The labourers had come into the harvest, recognizing with fresh eyes what it means to be baptized and rejoicing in it.[6] We must keep paying attention to the key issues and help people to see the benefits and the blessings which can come.

The final step is to help the people also to take responsibility for what is being done. Then the situation is not seen as something imposed on them, but something which they become glad to call their own. Heifetz calls it giving the work back to the people. This too may take a long time. In the example I have used, there will always be some who will never come to terms with such changes to their parish, but there will be others in due course who would not wish to go back to their former ways because they recognize and are grateful for what has happened. It is perhaps worth noticing as well one of the images Heifetz uses for this step: he anticipates Appleby when he says it 'frequently takes the form of orchestrating conflict'.[7] The orchestra leader returns.

This sketch hardly does justice to the subtlety of Heifetz's analysis, but these four steps offer a strategy which can begin to show those in leadership how to approach the demands their position places on them. By identifying the challenge, regulating the distress, and remaining attentive to the vital issues, and then by engaging people in the process so that they become responsible for it themselves, a person will not only be offering effective leadership, but also service. Here the leader is servant, as priests in particular are called to be. But the task is demanding. It may help if we consider some of the qualities such a person needs.

(vi)

I have mentioned Michael Hollings before.[8] He had been a Guards Officer during the Second World War and had been

6. Elsewhere it is different. Those who live in parts of the world which economically are far less prosperous and which have long been accustomed to the ministry of catechists, are witnessing an extraordinary growth in the numbers of ordained priests as well.
7. See Heifetz, *Leadership Without Easy Answers*, p. 262.
8. See above, pp. 4, 98–9.

decorated for bravery. In 1946 he came to Rome to study for the priesthood here at the Beda College where I am now rector. Later he was chaplain at Oxford. When he died, I was asked to contribute to a book which commemorates him and, while doing so, I came across an article he had written in 1950 for our College magazine, *The Beda Review*, shortly before he left Rome as a priest. It is called 'Some Notes on Leadership'. Very little has dated and I believe it has something to teach us here.[9]

Michael drew attention to three qualities in particular which he saw as vital for leadership. The first, he said, was humility, because 'to lead a man must be whole and human; he can only really be human if he is humble; because he can never have full confidence in himself unless he knows how very limited are his capabilities' (p. 21). This stress on being human endorses what we have recognized earlier as essential for priestly ministry.[10] It is instructive to find this direct reference in relation to leadership. Knowledge of our humanity shows us our limitations. We can't do everything. To use the earlier image, effective orchestra leaders cannot play every instrument in the orchestra; nobody can; it's not expected of them; but they must be able to talk the same language as the other members of the orchestra. In that way they gain their respect. People will follow gladly when they recognize the integrity and respect the competence of those in charge. Leaders are not expected to be experts at everything, but wise leaders know their limitations, while they have a sense of the larger picture and can co-ordinate it. Then those they lead trust them. They trust them because they recognize they are trusted by them. The humble leader, Michael argued, is ready to trust others and work with them. That certainly was his style. Life at the chaplaincy where later I was to follow him, was based

9. Michael Hollings, 'Some Notes on Leadership', *The Beda Review* (March 1950), pp. 20–7. See also Strange, 'Michael Hollings at Oxford', in Dalrymple, McCrimmon, and Tastard (eds.), *Press On! Michael Hollings, his Life and Witness* (Great Wakering, 2001), pp. 89–99.
10. See above, pp. 56–69.

upon it. He encouraged undergraduates to use their talents. He helped orchestrate their gifts.

The second quality Michael identified was courage, 'because', he observed, 'it often takes courage to delegate or to assume a new task' (p. 23). Sometimes when we trust, we are let down. Leadership is a risky business. Those who take seriously the demands of working collaboratively will know well what this involves. The courage Michael was meaning was not flashy, glamorous, or extrovert. He explained it in connection with fear. It was a lesson learnt in war. As he was to say later, 'I learnt that if you have cowardly instincts as I do, the only hope is to face the fear, the unknown, the threat.'[11] Courage can be needed in many situations. Let me offer a practical example.

While he was at Oxford, Michael wanted to make the chaplaincy secure financially. He suggested to the trustees who own it that they should raise or borrow enough money to buy some property which had come on the market and which, when refurbished, would become an asset. But the trustees felt that the risks involved were too great. What did Michael do? He said nothing more, but went and raised the money himself. Then, when the building had been refurbished, he gave it to the trustees. And what a valuable asset that property has proved to be. Here was courage. The risks foreseen by the trustees would have been as clear to Michael, but he decided to press on alone, taking responsibility for what he was doing. Those elements too – loneliness and taking responsibility – he mentioned as aspects of courage. We should not underestimate the sheer courage that can be required in many ways when we have to identify a challenge and regulate the distress it causes, while keeping the central issues in view and helping those we are leading and serving gradually to take responsibility for the outcome.

And the third quality Michael mentioned was generosity, which he described as 'coterminous with charity' (p. 25). Leader-

11. Hollings, *Living Priesthood* (Great Wakering, 1977), p. 20; see 'Some Notes on Leadership', p. 23.

ship calls for an enthusiasm which does not count the cost. The leader must lead from the front, not hide in the crowd or get lost at the rear. To be like that does not mean that the leader becomes dominant, treating all questions as though they were technical problems and supplying immediate answers from a presumed store of instant wisdom. The mark of this leadership is precisely generosity, an enthusiasm which gives a clear example, not by swamping others' gifts, but by encouraging their use. The leader does not just issue commands, but works at engaging others so that they share an understanding of the situation, become involved in the decisions which need to be made, and take responsibility for what has been decided. That is what true collaboration requires. It is demanding, time-consuming, and needs great patience. Such generosity is worthwhile because this way of working together is seen as being as valuable as achieving the objective. It's not just what you do; it's also the way you do it. When leadership is exercised as a service, it bears witness to a way of life shaped by the gospel.

(vii)

Humility, courage, and generosity, these are some of the qualities which those who find they have been called to lead must try to develop. And there is one other, not mentioned by Michael, but which is also essential, the ability to distinguish between the person and the role. Its importance is generally acknowledged, but it is not always easy to put into practice. We need to acquire the wisdom of the former Superior General of a friend of mine. When things were difficult and criticisms were being hurled at her, she was asked what she did. 'I duck,' she replied. In other words, she knew that what was being said was being aimed at her position as Superior General, and not at herself as a person. Sometimes, however, the situation can be more complex. The boundary between person and role may not be distinct, whether we consider the people we are working for or those we are working with.

Those we work for will approach us because we are professionals, but not for that reason alone. They sometimes hope for something more personal as well. They hope the care they receive will be warmed by friendship. How sad if that were not the case, if priests were not friendly with their parishioners. But it can be a minefield. It would be absurd to presume that everyone who approaches us is needy, obsessive, and clinging, but we live in a society so preoccupied with sexuality that it seems largely to have lost sight of friendship's value. Some care is needed. Innocent signals can be misinterpreted very easily. Ian McEwan's novel, *Enduring Love,* is the story of a man's life brought to the brink of disaster by such misinterpretation.[12] It explores territory which is all too familiar to those who have been ordained, even if their actual experience is less dramatic. And suspicions aroused by recent scandals have only made matters more obscure.

Then there are those we work with. A fine balance is necessary. We would hope to have friendly relationships with colleagues, but here too signals can go awry. Vicky Cosstick, who at the time was the co-ordinator for adult formation, RCIA, and catechesis for the Archdiocese of Southwark, gave a useful warning when she spoke to the National Conference of Priests in 1992. She observed:

> . . . it seems that priests know how to relate to other priests, and they know how to relate to lay people in a safe, hierarchical situation. Lay people, men and women both, also know how to manage 'signalling' among themselves. Similarly also with religious. But put them together and the boundaries and the signals go berserk. Signals are not given or received in a predictable manner.

She concludes: 'The only solution I know of is to keep the boundaries fairly tightly drawn in collaborative situations, at least

12. Ian McEwan, *Enduring Love* (London, 1997).

initially, and to focus on building relationship in the service of the task.'[13]

(viii)

Leaders who are servants must have the humility, courage, and generosity to immerse themselves in the impure. They should not be aloof. They ought to be friendly. At the same time, they must keep their sense of boundaries clear. And although leadership can be lonely, those who lead must not become isolated. It is a fine balancing act. The friends they have in any case become more vital and significant than ever. And they have to go on learning, because humble leaders realize that they don't know everything.

What has been said here about what it means to be both servant and leader, the different models, the strategy, and the qualities needed, is far from exhausting the subject. This role is as demanding as anything a priest is asked to do. Those of us who are ordained and who seek to orchestrate the gifts of others in order to help them meet the challenges with which they are faced and build up the Church, the people of God as the body of Christ, place ourselves under great pressure. How are we to cope? How can we put up with it? How can we endure it? At our ordination we have made a lifelong commitment. That too endures. It is time to consider in both senses enduring commitment.

13. Vicky Cosstick, 'The Experience of Collaboration', *Briefing*, vol. 22 (8 October 1992), p. 10.

12

Enduring Commitment

(i)

In 1997 I was invited to join the Working Party which had been set up by the Bishops' Conference of England and Wales and the National Conference of Priests to compose a report offering recommendations on Clergy Appraisal. Always a delicate issue and one which some opposed, nevertheless a sufficient consensus had gathered which felt the exercise would be helpful. It made a considered resource available for dioceses wishing to explore the issue. The report, which was published by the Catholic Media Office in 1999, was called *Supporting Ministry.* I mention it here for a particular reason. Meeting and reflecting regularly on ways of helping those who have been ordained to review their ministry and give an account of it, we soon realized that we had to avoid giving the impression that the only model of priesthood worth exercising was one which fulfilled an ideal radiant in every way. To quote Timothy Radcliffe just once more, he evoked what I have in mind with typical humour when addressing the National Conference of Priests in 2002. He remarked, 'The image of the priest in modern theology is so idealized that none of us can live up to it.' Then he explained, 'I read a lot in preparation for this lecture and I was horrified to discover that I had to be a brilliant preacher, an efficient administrator, a creative liturgical genius, a patient listener, an inspiring leader, a spiritual guru, good with the young and with the old.' And he observed, 'I became profoundly demoralized, and convinced that I was a bad priest who ought to apply for laicisation. You almost lost me.'[1] The point is well made. We are not required to attain some standard of absolute perfection. It is all right to be good enough. I would want to make the same point here.

The risk of discipleship should not be interpreted as a summons to perpetual and spectacular heroic valour. Which of us could manage to maintain such a way of living? The risk, as we have seen time and again, refers rather to a readiness to accept the consequences of the commitment we made when we were ordained, whatever they may be. Sometimes we may have to be heroic, but not always. Let me repeat what I have said before. Ministerial priesthood means that we are not negotiating, arranging everything on our own terms. We are prepared to be caught in the undertow, to be led where, left to ourselves, we would rather not go, to be square pegs in round holes, to play, when necessary, to our weaknesses rather than our strengths. The hallmark of that readiness is generosity, not spectacular achievement. The parable of the talents captures the idea neatly.

The story, of course, is well known (see Matthew 25:14–30). A man goes on a journey and, while he is away, he leaves various talents with his servants, five with one, two with another, one with the third. On his return he asks them to account for what he has given them. The servant who had been given five has made five more, and the servant with two two more, but the servant with one had simply buried it and now returns it. He is judged severely and condemned. More relevant here, however, is the treatment of the other two. They are treated exactly the same. The servant with five talents is praised no more than the servant with two; the servant with two is praised no less than the servant with five. What matters is not how skilled, talented, and gifted we may be, but that we exercise our skills,

1. Radcliffe, 'That your joy may be full', Address to the National Conference of Priests of England and Wales, September 2002, p. 2.

talents, and gifts with the utmost generosity. For all our limitations we give ourselves wholeheartedly to whatever is asked of us. It is that openness of heart which counts.

There may be fewer ordained priests in certain parts of the world today than there used to be, notably in Western Europe, the United States, and Australia, but there is no lack of generosity. Secular society may be prosperous, but it is not therefore automatically selfish and mean. There is plenty of evidence of extraordinary generosity. Charities fear charity fatigue, but show pictures on television of starving children or the devastation caused by earthquake, flood, or fire, and the response is regularly swift and admirable in its generosity. If generosity of heart is essential for ordained ministry, there is no shortage of the raw material. But we need to be aware of another Gospel scene as well.

There was the occasion when Jesus sat down opposite the treasury and watched people putting money into it. The rich put in large sums. Then we are told that 'a poor widow came, and put in two copper coins, which make a penny'. Jesus called his disciples and pointed her out to them. He told them, 'Truly, I say to you, this poor widow has put in more than all those who are contributing to the treasury. For they all contributed out of their abundance; but she out of her poverty has put in everything she had, her whole living' (Mark 12:41–4). Some are generous, but give from their excess, while the woman gave even from what little she had. Mother Teresa used to urge people, 'Give till it hurts.' Will we risk that hurt? When we find we might, we are getting ready to run the risk of discipleship.

The risk is a natural consequence of baptism, but it is the deliberately chosen path of those who offer themselves for ministerial priesthood. This theme too has become familiar. As we recognized earlier, those who have been ordained need the courage to face their own humanity, its flaws and failings as well as its strengths. Most of us are also asked to accept a call to be celibate, embracing solitude, but ready to accept loneliness too, while keeping the flame of love alive within us. We must give ourselves to prayerfulness and be prepared to study and explore the gospel message so as to proclaim it faithfully. In all these ways there may be times when we experience a sense of loss. We may have to pay a significant price. Risk is never far away for those who accept the call to discipleship and it leads us along our personal path to Calvary. What is essential is that we do not choose for ourselves. We are generous. We place ourselves in the Lord's hands and echo the prayer of Jesus in the garden, 'not my will but thine, be done' (Luke 22:42). When we choose to spend our lives in service, we are not seeking suffering. Suffering is not inevitable, but it is a risk we have to be prepared to take. Those who accept the call to serve must be prepared for sacrifice. We lay self-interest aside for the sake of others. We want to give without counting the cost. Who will walk this way?

(ii)

One answer, of course, is that many more would, if celibacy were not compulsory, or being a woman or being married were not a bar. We must not, however, fall into the trap of negotiating conditions. All the same these matters have been fiercely disputed.

Many will argue in favour of optional celibacy. While they will affirm the value of celibacy for the sake of the kingdom, they will also plead that the witness of a celibacy chosen freely has far greater value than celibacy imposed as part of a package. The point as it stands is unanswerable. When we contrast freedom and imposition, freedom must be prized more highly. Celibacy must be optional. At the same time, can I honestly claim that celibacy was imposed on me? No, I can't. I never thought I would just put up with it in order to be ordained. I can speak for no one except myself, but I suspect most of my contemporaries would say the same. It is true that I had no serious awareness of the implications of what I was undertaking, but many married people, whether the outcome has been happy or not, will say the same about their marriage. Our commitments involve decisions and the consequences are not always clear. That, as we know, is the nature of these risks which we run, and the unexpected does not invalidate the decision. Then, on the other hand, if celibacy is not a part of the package, how can it be a witness to the kingdom? If it is not a part of the package, how can people know whether those who have chosen celibacy, are truly committed to it? Perhaps they are gay? Or are they just natural bachelors? Celibacy, to echo Raymond Brown, has to be more than personal idiosyncrasy. Left to ourselves, we should all be reluctant celibates. We are not celibate because it suits us, but for the sake of the kingdom, because the love of Christ overwhelms us.

The ordination of women has been another controversial issue, especially in more recent times. The argument in the *Catechism of the Catholic Church*, however, is precise. It begins from a principle expressed in Canon Law: 'Only a baptized man (*vir*) validly receives sacred ordination' (*The Code of Canon Law*, can. 1024). The principle is based on what Jesus did. All his apostles were men and when they in their turn appointed successors those successors also were men. The *Catechism* then states crucially, 'The college of bishops, with whom the priests are united in the priesthood, makes the college of the twelve an ever-present and ever-active reality until Christ's return.' That statement supplies the kernel of the argument. What was first established, however conditioned, has acquired a status which cannot be changed. And so we have the conclusion: 'For this reason the ordination of women is not possible.' An intriguing sentence comes immediately before the conclusion: 'The Church recognizes herself to be bound by this choice made by the Lord himself' (*Catechism of the Catholic Church*, n. 1577). The sentence is intriguing because it seems to leave open the possibility that the Church might at some time review these arguments and no longer recognize that she was so bound. As matters stand, however, within the Catholic Church women cannot be ordained.[2]

And then there is the question of the ordination of married men. That, of course, has already started. At least from the time of Pope Pius XII, convert clergymen who were married, have been dispensed from the obligation of celibacy and been ordained as Catholic priests. Will that practice be extended? In his encyclical, *Ecclesia de Eucharistia*, Pope John Paul II emphasized vigorously the centrality of the eucharist in the life of a Christian community and described as distressing and irregular a situation in which there is no priest to lead it. He praised the laity and religious who tried to supply the lack, but described such a remedy as temporary. He urged everyone to pray for more vocations to the priesthood of the highest quality (see *Ecclesia de Eucharistia*, n. 32). Perhaps such vocations, wisely discerned, could come after all from among local married men who have already proved themselves by their unfailing generosity to their community.

It is possible to explore these issues, but important not to regard them as somehow supplying a solution to all the problems surrounding ministerial priesthood. If the Pope tomorrow were to make celibacy optional, reverse the decision about women's ordination, and allow married men to be ordained, the key questions would still have to be faced. We pick up the familiar threads. What does it mean for Jesus to be our master and friend and to follow him to the cross? Are we clear about the nature of ministerial priesthood, its development, and its essential difference from the universal priesthood, as well as its relationship with it? Have we understood this calling as a human calling? Are we committed to it as a vocation of love in which celibate loving has an inalienable role as a witness to the kingdom? Have

2. See Brian E. Ferme, 'The Response (28 October 1995) of the Congregation for the Doctrine of the Faith to the Dubium concerning the Apostolic Letter, *Ordinatio Sacerdotalis* (22 May 1994): Authority and Significance', *Periodica de Re Canonica* 85 (1996), pp. 689–727.

we grasped that we are to be people who live prayerfully, not just people who say prayers? Can we account for the hope that is in us? Have we braced ourselves for the great tasks laid on us of preaching the word, celebrating mysteries, and offering leadership as a service? Most of all, will we run the risk of discipleship, throw into the treasury our two copper coins, all we have to live on? These crucial, burning questions are there, irrespective of who and how many are ordained. It isn't a numbers game. We have made an enduring commitment and we must be ready to endure it.

(iii)

One particularly demanding feature of priestly life is its relentlessness. Most other people go home when they have finished the day's work. Home life can also be demanding, relationships fraught, children needy, domestic responsibilities exhausting. It is not all sweetness and light, but there is variety, the shift from one place to the other. Those who are ordained are usually living over the shop; there is no such variation and little respite. One friend of mine has described it as being like 'driving an articulated lorry up a slope'. How can we manage? How can we endure this enduring commitment?

One answer might refer to ongoing formation which is meant first of all to guide those who are ordained to grow in their understanding of who they are, 'seeing things with the eyes of Christ' (*Pastores Dabo Vobis*, n. 73). Then, secondly, it should help them not to lose sight of their purpose: they are to gather the church as a family in communion, to live more deeply the mystery of their relationship with Christ, and to increase their awareness of their share in the Church's saving mission (see *Pastores Dabo Vobis*, nn. 74–5). There is much truth in that and only fools would disregard the help that ongoing formation has to offer. We are never formed perfectly in this life. There is always more to be done, more to be learnt. But besides that we have to recognize that we do not maintain our commitment simply by acquiring more skills and polishing up further our talents, so as always to be able to give out more. We must realize as well that the ministry we offer is not all going one way. We also receive. In Daniel O'Leary's wise words, we 'do not pour out from [our] own fullness something to fill the empty spaces of those around [us]: rather do [we] draw out from the hearts and souls of those [we] are privileged to serve, the innate wisdom and beauty and healing already waiting to be released'.[3] As we minister to others, we find them ministering to us. Priests are called to serve the people, but they also renew us. They do so even as we carry out those tasks with which we are identified most plainly.

(iv)

Consider preaching. Those who are ordained are servants of the word. As we know well, it is the first of the tasks laid upon us. Here most clearly it might seem that we give rather than receive. But wise experience soon teaches us something different: those who will no longer learn can no longer teach. So, when a couple comes to prepare for their wedding, whether devoted churchgoers or not, I have always given them a copy of the wedding ceremony which includes the selection of readings for marriages from the Lectionary. I ask them to choose the readings they want. Then, at a later session, we discuss the reasons for their choice. My homily can find its direction from that conversation. They have not determined what I will say, but they influence it. I am learning from them. Of course, I have well-tried ways of expressing certain ideas, but I am never just recycling 'the wedding homily' throughout the marriage season. Each one is fresh and its novelty refreshes me.

Again, when someone dies in the parish, we visit the family

3. Daniel J. O'Leary, *New Hearts for New Models: a spirituality for priests* (Dublin, 1997), p. 56.

and listen to the stories they tell. That is common practice. Their friends call or write and gradually a picture of the person emerges which develops and deepens the knowledge I may already have. Then, when I preach at the funeral, I can draw upon what I have learnt. The structure of the homily may be one I commonly use, especially if my knowledge of the dead person is slight, but the content is personal. And so I have often found myself, in spite of sadness, encouraged in the exercise of my ministry. The source of that encouragement has been the people.

Weddings and funerals, of course, are special occasions, but Sunday by Sunday, even day by day, we can find ourselves renewed when we preach, provided we are not delivering from on high, but listening to and learning from and responding to the people whom we have been called to serve.

Then consider the sacraments we celebrate, especially the sacraments of healing. First, there is the sacrament of reconciliation. We all have our dark periods and there have been times in the past when I have felt down, but then have found myself revived by hearing confessions. To sit in the confessional and listen to men and women as they humbly and sadly acknowledge their sins and failings and seek a better way, is an extraordinary privilege. People sometimes ask, 'Isn't hearing confessions depressing?' Sometimes it may be, but usually it is inspiring. Now the numbers using individual confession are in decline, but services of reconciliation have also brought me a sense of new life. It is wonderful to see a church filled with people, rapt in prayer, quietly examining their consciences, and then approaching the priest. It is deeply moving to witness their unmistakable goodness as they confess.

And then there is the care of the sick. Pope John Paul anointed some of them in Southwark Cathedral on his visit to Britain in 1982. He caught the moment precisely, when he observed: 'We begin by imagining that we are giving [to those who are sick and handicapped]; we end by realizing that they have enriched us.'[4] Pilgrims to Lourdes will know just what he means and so will many others for whom the care of those who are sick is a daily responsibility. As we minister to people in one way, we discover that they also are ministering to us.

Leadership too, we have seen, especially when it means influencing a community to face its problems, to handle the challenges and the changes which confront it, is not exercised effectively from afar. Leaders are servants. They must not hold themselves aloof, but instead have to take their place as a part of the community. However, that does not solve everything. Problems, we noticed, may be either technical, practical and particular, requiring a specific decision, or they may be adaptive, complex and challenging, and needing to be discussed. If everyone agrees on which kind of problem it is, all should be well, but sometimes they will disagree. Is this some particular matter or a more complex challenge? Is it a time for decision or discussion? There can be conflict which may be severe. At this time, the last thing we feel is renewed. It may be tempting to regress into dictatorship or irresponsible delegation. But if we persevere in working with people, there will be a sense of renewal, because our ministry will be deeply in tune with the gospel. As we work with others, we find we are invigorated; we come through with them to new life.

The way we engage with people in the very exercise of our ministry, preaching, celebrating sacraments, and leading, renews us. It is not merely that the ministry is satisfying; the people we are serving are also ministering to us.

The relationships we form as we work, which can be a source of comfort and strength, may not only be professional; at times they are also personal, and that is a blessing. In some situations, there may be a danger of blurred boundaries, but not inevitably. Those who befriend us are a treasure; they keep us human. A ministry without love will wither and die. And then there are the friends we make independently of our work.

4. *The Pope in Britain: collected speeches and homilies* (Slough, 1982), p. 24.

One summer holiday in the sixties, when I was a student, I first read Peter Brown's life of Augustine. There I discovered that Augustine grew up in a circle in which company and the intimacy of friendship were taken for granted. As the demands of his ministry developed, however, he found himself separated more and more from those who were dear to him and that separation became one of the keen burdens of his later life.[5] There can be circumstances beyond our control. In various ways it can happen to any of us. It has happened to me. The benefits of working in Rome are tempered by the inaccessibility of so many of my friends. And yet their friendship, even at this distance, sustains and supports me. It is a guarantee of help, a source of encouragement, a comfort in difficulty. My friends offer a promise of merriment, good talk, wise advice, and generous hospitality. Some are ordained, but naturally the majority are not. Very many are not Catholics. I hold them in love and believe I am loved by them. They do not diminish the ministry I offer. They are pure gift for which I give constant thanks. They help my commitment to endure.

(v)

People speculate about the future of ministerial priesthood, but, whatever the future may hold, to be ordained is to run the risk of discipleship. That risk, as we have seen, can take many forms and may take many more. If we are to understand this priesthood, however, we need to keep our eyes on those who have lived it faithfully. They have so much to teach us.

In 1990 Fr Patrick Rorke died. I had known Pat Rorke for more than thirty years and John Harriott, who had known him much longer, devoted his next 'Periscope' column in *The Tablet* to him. He said of Pat, 'One such man, one such priest, is worth a thousand paragraphs of clotted abstractions about Priesthood.'

5. See Peter Brown, *Augustine of Hippo: a biography* (London, 1975), pp. 155–6, 161, 209–11, 324–5.

He called his article, 'A Priest to Remember'.[6] So what made Pat Rorke so memorable?

John came to know Pat when Pat had returned from a Japanese prison camp after the Second World War. He was invited to go and serve his mass while Pat was recuperating. The tall, well-built, dignified figure, familiar to those of us who knew him later, at that time only weighed six or seven stone, was crumpled and haggard, and had to say mass sitting down. Over the next couple of years, John wrote, they spent many hours in conversation. He explained, 'Pat did most of the talking – about God, the Society of Jesus, life in the camps, his school life at Mount St Mary's, his family; but most of all about people he had known and the life of the spirit.' And he remarked, 'I had never been so close to a priest and I thought I knew everything important about him.'

And he continued:

> Then one day in the 1960s I called in at a Raynes Park barber's shop. The barber asked me if I knew Fr Pat Rorke. 'Yes', I said, 'do you?' 'I was a POW with him in Java', he answered. And he went on to tell me all that Pat had never spoken about; of the effect he had had on morale, of the inspiration he had been, of the courage he had shown when he voluntarily took beatings and accepted other indignities in place of men too weak to endure them. In the eyes of the barber he had been a solid gold hero. Later I met other men who shared that view. Though I respected his reticence, from then on it was a side of Pat I could never forget, even when he seemed a most unlikely hero . . .
>
> Pat was a hero but not a plaster saint. He could be inconsiderate, garrulous, sentimental and vain in childish ways . . . But what he was above all was a man, a priest, a Jesuit with an absolute passion for God. He was a God-filled man, a Christ enthusiast, as other men are enthusiasts

6. John F.X. Harriott, 'A Priest to Remember', *The Tablet*, 15 September 1990.

> for politics or cars or cricket. Everything he saw, experienced, felt, was related to God and it spilled out in conversation as another man's conversation might keep circling back to his family or his business . . . Perhaps, like other enthusiasts, he sometimes went over the top. But it came from a core of faith so deep and real, it made God real and even the most unlikely listeners take Him seriously. It also made one realise what being a priest is really about.
>
> Pat was a priest, not at all a cleric. He cared nothing for status, nothing for caste, had nothing of the official about him, and not a touch of professional pomposity. He was not at all trendy, and not a natural flag-carrier for causes. But nor was he narrow-minded or censorious. He saw his business as to make the mercy, the charity and the caring strength of Almighty God a living reality in as many lives as possible, and most of all wherever there was pain, trouble and affliction.
>
> It drove him to travel up and down the land to be wherever he thought encouragement and hope were needed. It made everyone he met feel special to him because they were. His own faith and hope were a source of infectious healing. Exasperating he may often have been, embarrassing sometimes, but I doubt whether he ever left a household not feeling for his presence and his wisdom better about themselves, better about life and its conditions, stronger in faith and richer in hope. Of course he was not unique; but he was a marvellous example of a rare breed.

And so the conclusion: 'One such man, one such priest, is worth a thousand paragraphs of clotted abstractions about Priesthood.' Here without doubt was a priest who served the Lord with joy.

I take this tribute out from time to time and read it. It never fails to stir and move me. It captures Pat magnificently. I knew him from the time I was at school. We exchanged letters occasionally. I visited him at Loyola Hall, the Jesuit Retreat House near Rainhill, and we met last when he was Spiritual

Director at Oscott College, the seminary for the Archdiocese of Birmingham. He had come to my ordination.

I was ordained on 21 December 1969. It was the Fourth Sunday of Advent, but the Gospel reading for that date, when it falls on a weekday, is the account of Mary's visitation to her cousin Elizabeth. I listen to it and hear Elizabeth's words, 'blessed is she who believed that the promise made her by the Lord would be fulfilled' (Luke 1:45 Jerusalem Bible). Pat believed the promise made to him would be fulfilled. Overwhelming promises are made to those who accept the call to be ordained and run the risk of discipleship: 'every one who has left houses or brothers or sisters or father or mother or children or lands, for my name's sake, will receive a hundredfold, and inherit eternal life' (Matthew 19:29). Blessed are those who believe that the promise made them by the Lord will be fulfilled.

Index

Main discussions are indicated in italics